THE BORGIAS

Lust for power was the force that drove the Borgias to bribery, torture and murder. From obscure Spanish origins the family rose to control the papacy, one of the most influential power centres of Renaissance Europe.

Alonso inhabited the Vatican for only three years, but a combination of patience and cunning eventually produced a second Borgia pope, who placed his illegitimate children Cesare and Lucrezia in positions of great wealth and power. Rodrigo's twelve years as Pope Alexander VI were distinguished by corruption and scandal on an unprecedented scale.

Harry Edgington evokes all the excitement and daring of the Borgias as he chronicles the forging of an amazing dynasty.

THE BORGIAS

Harry Edgington

Hamlyn Paperbacks

THE BORGIAS
ISBN 0 600 20318 2

First published in Great Britain 1981
by Hamlyn Paperbacks

Copyright © 1981 by Harry Edgington

Hamlyn Paperbacks are published by
The Hamlyn Publishing Group Ltd,
Astronaut House,
Feltham,
Middlesex, England

(Paperback Division: Hamlyn Paperbacks,
Banda House, Cambridge Grove,
Hammersmith, London W6 0LE)

Printed and bound in Great Britain by
Cox & Wyman Ltd, Reading

To Pat and Rita

Contents

1

ALONSO DE BORJA, FOUNDER OF THE DYNASTY

Alonso de Borja was born into a family of opportunistic adventurers who had been granted lands in Spain as a reward for helping to free Valencia from the colonizing yoke of the Moors, the Islamic marauders who ruled much of the Iberian peninsula from the eighth to the thirteenth century. A long-standing family tradition held that they were descended from the Aragon royal line, but this was untrue – because they did not have an illustrious background, the Borjas had invented one. They were, however, landed gentry who could claim the respect accorded to provincial nobility. Alonso's father, Domingo, was a farmer, though he did not actually work the fields himself. He was a minor country gentleman of little importance.

The boy spent his early years in the family home, a castle dominating the dusty town of Torre de Canals, set in the foothills of the mountains south of Valencia, in the Spanish kingdom of Aragon. He was a lonely youngster, spending most of his time immersed in reading and study. By adolescence, a natural teaching gift within him flowered and he became unofficial schoolmaster to the town's peasant children.

At the age of fourteen, the precociously-learned Alonso was sent to study at the University of Lerida, the city which served as the official residence for the kings of Aragon. He wisely decided to study civil and church law, which embraced the two most potent forces of the day. Not unexpectedly, he was a brilliant student. His sharp mind and tenacious temperament saw him quickly taking doctorates in his chosen subjects, and he stayed on at the university as a lecturer.

A natural piety marked Alonso's early years, and was to be a trademark for the rest of his life. He was often seen, a lone figure at silent prayer, in the chapels of Lerida or near his home town. He seems to have drifted into church life more by accident than design, although his chosen course may have been influenced by a meeting he had with Vincent Ferrer, a Dominican friar, in Valencia when he was about twenty. Ferrer was a wandering preacher, a charismatic, fiery man, with a flowing beard and penetrating eyes. A masterly and emotional speaker, his black-robed presence in a church, a cathedral, or in a public square always guaranteed a full house and an overflow congregation crowding the windows and rooftops of surrounding houses. Calling for penitence and threatening God-sent disasters, his one-man evangelical crusade carried his fame before him as he diverted souls from eternal damnation in tours of Spain, France, and Italy.

Alonso heard he was coming to Valencia and went to the ancient walled city to hear Ferrer's particular burning brand of Christianity. After Ferrer had finished preaching, Alonso walked up to meet him and ask that he should be remembered in prayers. Ferrer, so Alonso later recounted to his friends, seemed affected by the young man and told him, 'My son, I rejoice with you. Remember that you are destined one day to be the ornament of your country and your family. You will be invested with the highest authority to which mortal man can attain. I myself, after my death, will be an object of your veneration. Strive to keep yourself in your present virtuous life.' Now it was Alonso's turn to be affected. He stood, transfixed, staring. Then Ferrer's piercing gaze caused him to lower his eyes. The friar smiled, nodded confirmation of his prediction, and walked off. Alonso took his words to mean that one day he would become pope. He was never to forget this prophecy.

Alonso followed Ferrer's advice and a few years later the Spanish anti-pope, Benedict XIII – one of three men in Christendom at the time claiming to be the successor of St Peter – appointed him a canon of the cathedral of Lerida. Benedict and his rival claimants were the product of the

10

Great Schism, an event which appeared likely to shatter the whole order of the Catholic Church. Alonso was to spend much of his life trying to heal the resultant wound.

The year of Alonso's birth, 1378, had also seen the beginning of the Great Schism. The elderly Pope Gregory XI died in March and a few days later sixteen cardinals had gathered in the Vatican to elect his successor. Their conclave was put under siege by an angry, demanding, sword-waving mob. Rome was a wild and lawless city then, which was the main reason that recent popes had prudently decided to base themselves in the comparative safety of the French city of Avignon. Fear of the rampaging crowd induced the Sacred College to choose the Archbishop of Bari, Bartolomeo Prignano, as the new pope. He had two distinct advantages, as they saw it. He was Italian, and he was not one of them.

After the conclave, the cardinals had fled from Rome and Archbishop Prignano rode into the city to reign as Pope Urban VI. The church might have accepted him if he had not alarmed the establishment by trying to shake up the existing order, bludgeoning through pet reforms in a high-handed, authoritarian manner. He bridled at resistance to his demands and threatened to create sufficient Italian cardinals to dominate the Vatican political machine, so his countrymen could outvote his opposition. The cardinals who had chosen Prignano declared his election invalid because it had been forced on them by threats of the Roman crowd. Then they formed another conclave to elect one of their number, Robert of Geneva, as Pope Clement VII. The new pope took an army to Rome, aiming to drive out Urban VI, but Clement was, surprisingly, repulsed. He retired to Avignon where he set up court in the old Pontifical Palace which had been utilized as an alternative Vatican by popes wary of disordered Rome.

This fiasco had left two popes with much in common. Both had been elected by the same Sacred College. Both had been chosen unanimously. And when the rival popes died, each was followed by an elected successor. Europe found itself split in support of one or the other. A Spanish cardinal, Pedro de Luna, succeeded to the Avignon papacy, and ruled as Benedict XIII. When he became as unpopular as Urban VI had been, Benedict was hounded into exile and based himself in Aragon.

In 1409 a council was set up in Pisa to resolve the papal issue. After due deliberation, the two reigning popes were declared deposed, and the Greek Archbishop of Milan, Pietro Filigaris, was designated Pope Alexander V. Unfortunately but not surprisingly, the two other popes refused to recognize the authority of the legislators at Pisa. Each asserted his own legality, as did the new claimant – which meant that, instead of two, now there were three popes, each declaring himself the legal pontiff, and each with his own formidable body of supporters. In 1415, another church council set out to persuade the trio of popes to relinquish their authority. Two agreed, but Benedict, in his now familiar intransigent style, adamantly refused. So the council announced him deposed. Benedict sneered at the decision and locked himself away in an impregnable fortress on the Peniscola peninsula on the Mediterranean coast. From there, he continued to issue papal decrees which were loyally adhered to by his Spanish supporters.

The Aragon delegate to this latest church council was Alonso de Borja. But, at the behest of the new and youthful King of Aragon, Alfonso V, Alonso did not attend. For the king had swiftly realized he could make some valuable political capital by threatening to support Benedict against Martin V, the pope who sat in Rome. King Alfonso succeeded in extorting a series of concessions from the official pontiff, gaining for himself the greater share of church revenues raised in Aragon and the right to hand out church offices.

Shortly after, Alonso de Borja was sent by his chapter in Lerida to negotiate the finances of the diocese with royal officials. Alonso's abilities came to the notice of the king, who immediately saw the value of harnessing such a lucid intelligence to royal advantage. King Alfonso persuaded Alonso to switch sides and made the young lawyer his personal secretary, chief counsellor, and confidential adviser on foreign affairs, particularly in dealings with the Holy See in Rome.

In 1423 Benedict died, but left a schismatic legacy. He had created four cardinals and one of them, Jean Carrier, was elected Clement VIII. The new rival pope was crowned amidst much pomp and ceremony, at King Alfonso's express instructions. It was his way of showing Pope Martin where the power lay in his kingdom. King Alfonso continued playing this game until a new ambition diverted him.

The southern Italian state of Naples had long been a prize sought by his family, and Alfonso launched a diplomatic and military campaign to gain the country for his dynasty. Alonso de Borja spotted the opportunity for a deal. So he persuaded King Alfonso to support Martin, and in return the pope backed his claim to the Neapolitan throne. Which left only the problem of Clement VIII, who had shut himself away on Peniscola and was not interested in promoting Alfonso's dynastic dreams. The king passed the problem over to the loyal and reliable Alonso, who went to see Pope Clement in 1429. A subtle combination of threats and promises persuaded Clement that his best prospect lay in relinquishing his share of the papacy and accepting the consolation prize of the Bishopric of Majorca. Clement's cardinals then held a conclave to solemnly elect as pope the man who had performed that role for some years – Martin V.

King Alfonso, delighted that his bridges to Rome had been repaired, wanted Alonso rewarded with a cardinalate for his work in healing the Great Schism. However, grateful as Martin was to Alonso, he recognized that the move was a political ploy, and that King Alfonso was seeking an enlargement of his own power by having his formidable ally placed in the Sacred College of Cardinals. Instead the pope conveyed his gratitude by elevating Alonso to the prestigious and valuable position of Bishop of Valencia. A small impediment stood in the way of this course, however. Alonso, though trained in church law, was not even a priest. King Alfonso overcame this obstacle by arranging for his ordination. The next day, the papal ambassador to Aragon,

Cardinal Pierre de Foix, supervised Alonso's enthronement as bishop.

Alonso, who had once worked ardently to secure support for the schismatic Benedict papacy, had to perform a masterful about-turn in order to persuade Valencia to accept the new order of things. With a sure theatrical air, he mounted colourful and ostentatious religious ceremonies. He had holy relics brought to the cathedral in Valencia and started work on a building to house them. These were not the acts of a completely cynical man, for Alonso genuinely believed in the stabilizing power of a united papacy. He did, however, make sure that the healing moment coincided with the most propitious time for his king.

Now in his fifties, he had become King Alfonso's chief confidant. It was he who stepped in to resolve quarrels with neighbouring monarchs, and he who sat on the Council of Regency as Vice-Chancellor when Alfonso was leading his armies in Naples. In 1432, the king called Alonso away from his church duties to help plan the restructuring of Naples. Alonso remained at his side during the conquest of that country as the king's trusted right-hand man, a true power behind the throne. It was Alonso who was entrusted with the task of escorting Ferrante, the King's illegitimate son, from Aragon to Naples.

When King Alfonso rode in triumph into the city of Naples in 1442, Alonso was at his side. The task of reorganising the judicial system of the newly-won kingdom was placed in Alonso's capable hands, and he was made President of the Royal Council and of the tribunal responsible for religious affairs. He was also appointed tutor to the young Ferrante, soon to be crowned King of Naples. The reigning pope, Eugenius IV, was persuaded by Alonso to bow to the inevitable and agree to the change of dynasty in the land of Naples, which was, nominally at least, still a papal fief. In return, King Alfonso guaranteed his undivided allegiance to the pope and promised help in setting up a crusade aimed at reclaiming the Holy Land from the Turks.

To mark the end of the antipathy between the papacy and

King Alfonso, Eugenius agreed to make Alonso a cardinal. Vincent Ferrer, the wandering friar, had died some years before but his prophecy, so outrageous when it was made, now moved into the realm of the possible.

The sixty-six-year-old Alonso abruptly abandoned his state duties and went to live in Rome, which was still partly in ruins after the catastrophes of the Dark and Middle Ages. The entire population of the city was served by the one aqueduct left standing by the Goths a thousand years before. Unused churches were crumbling from neglect, and the Roman forum was being used as a cattle pasture. Allocated the Roman parish of Quattro Coronati, Alonso was to lead a quiet and secluded life as a cardinal for the next eleven years. In vivid contrast to his days in the Spanish court, he studiously avoided the political intrigues which permeated the papal court. He concentrated his efforts on restoring his cardinal's palace, paying for it out of his bishop's income. Showing a marked disdain for luxury, any surplus funds he had were channelled into support for hospitals and the destitute of Rome. His life of pious austerity marked him out from his colleagues in the Sacred College, who were wont to indulge in the more worldly pleasures offered to them in the city. Many had mistresses or concubines, and their own children. Not Alonso. He shone as a fine example of dignified piety.

He played no part in the behind-the-scenes dealings which marked the election of Nicholas V, acknowledged as the first of the Renaissance popes, in 1447. Observers concluded that the master diplomatist had decided to enjoy a tranquil retirement after an eventful career. In reality, Alonso nursed a secret and fervent ambition to see the prophecy of Vincent Ferrer fulfilled. He did not know how this was to come about, but he was content to wait for fate to call, as it always had before.

His appointment with destiny came when the cardinals gathered in conclave to elect the successor to Nicholas V in 1455. Alonso de Borja was by then seventy-seven years old and in poor health. He was not even considered a candidate.

However, the conclave reached a stalemate, split between the rival claims of the representatives of the Colonnas and the Orsinis, the two most powerful families of the Romagna, the region around Rome which comprised most of what remained of the ancient papal States. Then the very impediments which had been deemed to disqualify Alonso commended him to the cardinals as the most acceptable pope. The Colonnas and the Orsinis reasoned that Alonso was too sickly to affect their power and, in any event, would not live very long. They were to be proved dramatically wrong on both counts.

The royal courts of Europe were astounded when they heard of Alonso's election as Pope Calixtus III. The only person not surprised was the new pope himself, who had been confidently awaiting the moment when he would fulfil the prophecy of Vincent Ferrer. In one of his first acts as pope, Calixtus ordained that Ferrer should be elevated to sainthood. It was his way of thanking the Dominican preacher.

King Alfonso was delighted at the prospect of a man who owed him so much being seated on the throne of St Peter. Along with the other monarchs of Christendom, he expected Calixtus to be a pliable puppet, eager to respond to Aragon royal interests. The new pope quickly made it abundantly clear that he was, and would remain, independent. His attitude was a rude shock to Alfonso, and resulted in a conflict which was to last for the rest of their lives.

Age had certainly weakened Calixtus's body, but this was a surface illusion. Underneath that frail exterior, his spirit was as robust and vibrant as ever. Within days of his election, Calixtus demonstrated his vitality when the procession taking him to his coronation was obstructed by a brawl between younger members of the Orsini and Colonna families. He called in the heads of the families for an audience in which he ordered them to control their relatives. They were stunned by this display of unexpected and undesired papal authority.

As absolute monarch of the Papal States, set among the

patchwork of rival dukedoms, principalities, kingdoms, and republics which made up the land known as Italy, Calixtus enjoyed a surfeit of temporal power, bolstered by the ever-present threat of the much-feared papal excommunication. Almost permanently bed-ridden by gout, he spent much of his reign propped up in a shuttered and candle-lit bedroom. But this did not stop him handling a prodigious workload. He insisted on personally examining all the church documents which passed through his offices, diminishing the power of the Apostolic Protonotaries, the Vatican officials allowed to sign papal decrees. His ascetic nature meant he was unwilling to follow the example of Pope Nicholas and heap financial support on the artists and writers of the dawn of the Renaissance.

He ignored the bitterness surrounding him and turned to the project which was to dominate his three-year papacy: a Christian crusade against the Moslem Turks, who had recently conquered Constantinople and were threatening to overrun Europe. Calixtus saw himself as a Knight of the Cross, entrusted with the holy purpose of driving the Turks from Christendom. He authorized a collection throughout the church of a 'Turkish tithe', and dreamed of raising an army and a fleet to retake Constantinople in an amphibious assault, then to set about a systematic destruction of the Ottoman Empire. It was to remain just a dream, even though European princes vied with each other to make sacred promises of support. Their pledges turned out to be worthless. The crusade represented a medieval concept to them and they were, in any event, too busy struggling for European land to allow a Middle East adventure to distract them. King Alfonso was invested with the Emblem of the Cross and agreed to raise funds in Aragonese and Neapolitan churches to help finance the crusade. He used the money to build a fleet, but the ships, instead of sailing against the Turks, were flung into an assault on the northern Italian city-state of Genoa. Calixtus never forgot his old master's treachery, and was never to forgive him.

To encourage French support for the crusade, Calixtus

agreed to order an urgent re-examination of the case of Joan of Arc, who had been burned at the stake twenty-four years earlier after being found guilty of heresy by a church court. A papal court dutifully overruled that verdict and declared her a saint. But the ploy failed to engender French assistance. Undeterred, Calixtus financed his crusade by plundering the papal treasury and selling off church possessions. The Vatican's gold and silver tableware disappeared into the melting pots, to be replaced by plain earthenware. Within months of his accession Calixtus had raised enough money to build a squadron of galleys, which was entrusted to the command of Pietro Urrea, Archbishop of Tarragona, who was ordered to drive the Turks from the western Mediterranean in preparation for the overland invasion. Urrea, however, soon became bored with his task and switched to piracy, seizing and looting any ships he came across. Calixtus, inundated with complaints about the rogue archbishop, realized he would not trust him either.

An assault on the papal city of Siena by a rebel Venetian soldier, Jacapo Piccinino, diverted Calixtus's attention from his crusade. He sent a church army under the command of the Count of Ventimiglia to deal with Piccinino, who hoped to carve out estates for himself in central Italy. But the count switched sides, and only a massive bribe, taken from funds earmarked for the crusade, persuaded Piccinino to give up the city.

This treacherous betrayal was the final disappointment for Calixtus. Convinced that he could only rely on members of his own family, he started wholesale recruitment of them into important church posts. To ensure their continued and unswerving devotion to the Borja cause, he generously rewarded them with valuable lands and estates.

From the first days of his papacy, Calixtus had eased relatives from his native district into comfortable positions in the Vatican bureaucracy. His nephew, Rodrigo de Borja, had followed him to Italy and studied canon law at the University of Bologna. He had been appointed Apostolic Protonotary and assigned a number of other minor but lucrative church posts, including the absentee deanship of a parish in Aragon. Another nephew, Luis Juan de Mila, was given the post of Bishop of Segorbe, a provincial Spanish town. The church positions, though paying good salaries, involved no work and did not even require their holders' presence.

Now Calixtus's thinly disguised nepotism became blatantly obvious. Rodrigo's brother, Pedro Luis de Borja, was called to Rome and given the Count of Ventimiglia's post as Captain-General of the Church, the command of the papal armed forces. He was also assigned the governorship of twelve papal cities which dominated strategic strongholds in the Papal States and Tuscany. Rodrigo and Luis Juan de Mila, though both only in their twenties, were then created cardinals. This move astounded the other members of the Sacred College, who only agreed to it because they were still expecting the ailing Calixtus to die at any time, and hopefully before the appointments could be confirmed.

Rodrigo was dispatched as Legate to one of the Papal States, the March of Ancona, to deal with a rebellion. Using a mixture of force and persuasion, Rodrigo quickly brought peace to the whole region. Calixtus was so impressed with the success of the mission and his nephew's display of administrative ability that when Rodrigo returned to Rome he was made Vice-Chancellor of the Church, the most powerful position in the Vatican hierarchy after the pope. As an added bonus and mark of his gratitude, Calixtus resigned from the Bishopric of Valencia and bequeathed the valuable position to Rodrigo.

But Pedro Luis de Borja, handsome, hot-blooded and proud, was the apple of Calixtus's eye and the man the elderly pope felt was destined to fulfil his dynastic dreams. As Captain-General of the Church, Pedro Luis was given the task of subduing and controlling the nobility who held castles and land in Rome and the Romagna, the strategically vital north-eastern section of the Papal States, nominally on behalf of the pope, and whose power had grown while absentee pontiffs ruled. This same nobility found themselves eased out

19

of their seats of influence in the Vatican by Calixtus's familial administration. They were not pleased by this unwelcome attention. Calixtus shrewdly played off the Orsini and Colonna families against each other to establish his hegemony over them. His method was to divide and rule. On the one hand he tended to favour the Colonna, knowing he could then rely on them to help him whip the rival Orsini into line. When Pedro Luis was appointed Prefect of Rome and Commandant of the Castel Sant'Angelo, the impregnable papal fortress alongside the River Tiber, the Orsini knew conclusively that their days were numbered, for the posts had traditionally been filled by one of their number. Calixtus directed Pedro Luis to hound the remaining Orsini from Rome, then join with the Colonna-led forces to take over the fortresses to which the Orsini had fled for refuge. Pedro Luis was brutally successful in carrying out this mission, which earned the arrogant young man the undying hatred of the Orsini. This laid the foundation for a family feud which was to last for many decades.

Anyone who showed even flickering opposition to the Borja will felt the instant and dangerous wrath of Calixtus. After the débâcle of the crusader squadron under Pietro Urrea, a new fleet of thirty ships was fitted out and sailed under the nominal command of the Vatican Chamberlain, Cardinal Scarampo. But Scarampo unwisely voiced the opinion that, as an anti-Borja man, he was being shunted away from the centre of power. So Calixtus called up three more relatives, Juan and Miguel de Borja – both of whom had commanded vital papal fortresses – and Juan Lanzol, to sail as galley captains and 'assist' Cardinal Scarampo. They were the pope's eyes and ears in the fleet with orders, if they deemed it necessary, to usurp Scarampo's command. Calixtus's dream of hurling the fleet against Constantinople was, however, far beyond its realistic capability and Scarampo, backed by his watchful aides, contented himself with sporadic attacks on the Turkish garrisons in Greece and the islands of the Aegean.

King Alfonso was the next to feel the heat of Calixtus's

disapproval. Incredibly, the pope claimed that the Aragonese monarch had long been a problem to the church – when it was Calixtus himself who had stage-managed the interminable conflicts. A battle raged between them because Alfonso chose to bestow wealthy church offices on relatives. Calixtus was angry at this because he wanted the posts for his own kinfolk. He fumed, 'Let the King of Aragon rule his own realm, and leave the task of governing the church to us!' Alfonso, hungry for more territory, sought control of the March of Ancona, but was thwarted when Rodrigo de Borja brought the state to heel. So he gave his support to both the Orsini and the rebel soldier Piccinino in his attack on Siena.

When Alfonso wanted his eleven-year-old illegitimate grandson – the offspring of Ferrante, his illegitimate son who ruled Naples – made Archbishop of Saragossa, he approached Calixtus. In the face of a thunderous refusal, Alfonso threatened to withdraw his support for Calixtus's papacy. Calixtus reciprocated by holding a counter-threat of excommunication over Alfonso's head. Later the king's mistress, the beautiful Lucrezia d' Alagno, called on Calixtus to ask, unsuccessfully, for Alfonso to be given a papal dispensation so they might marry. Undeterred by his former collaborator's intransigence, King Alfonso tried to persuade Calixtus to confirm Ferrante's hereditary claim to the throne of Naples. Calixtus responded by asserting that Naples was still a papal fief. Far from acceding to Alfonso's request, he declared that he was personally investigating the claim that the French royal line made to Naples. There was a very real fear, he said, that Aragon and France would go to war over the succession. To avoid this, he declared, he was considering taking the Neapolitan throne back into church custody. Alfonso was speechless with rage, for he, like the rulers of Italy's numerous states, knew the real reason behind Calixtus's recalcitrant attitude over the Neapolitan throne. He was scheming to declare it vacant, prior to sequestering it for his favourite nephew, Pedro Luis de Borja.

The tentacles of the Borja family had acquired a stranglehold on the church. Calixtus sat on the papal throne.

Rodrigo, as Vice-Chancellor, controlled the government. Pedro Luis, as Captain-General, commanded the armies and castle strongholds. Their position seemed impregnable. But it was not. They were secure only as long as Calixtus lived. The old man had shown he still possessed a nimble mind and could call on seemingly unlimited reserves of energy when it came to advancing his family's fortunes. But he could not last for ever. And the first signs that the end was approaching for him came in the summer of 1458, while he was trying to dupe the French into assisting him in a military campaign to wrest the Neapolitan crown from Ferrante.

The young man was feeling somewhat vulnerable since the death of his father, King Alfonso, a short while before. The French were, however, wary of this prospective involvement. For they feared, correctly, that Calixtus was planning to use them with the false promise of handing the throne over to their nominee. They, too, knew of his heady ambitions for Pedro Luis. His constant scheming and undiminished hopes for the crusade had kept Calixtus in Rome during July, when the clammy humidity sapped the strength of even the strongest men. He fell gravely ill and retired to his shuttered bedroom in the Vatican. Premature rumours that he had died spread and the cardinals started laying plans for the political struggle which lay ahead.

By the beginning of August, it was clear that Calixtus could not last much longer. But the ailing pope was ignoring the inevitable. He talked on and on about his plans for the crusade, issuing an order that church bells should be rung every day at noon to remind Christians of their duty to pray for its success. He also announced that he wanted to appoint a batch of new cardinals, and assigned the papal cities of Benevento, Terracina, and Civitavecchia to Pedro Luis's control. Benevento and Terracina were marooned within the territory of Naples and garrisoned by Ferrante's troops. How Pedro Luis was intended to take control of these cities was a problem which did not seem to occur to Calixtus's wandering mind.

Pedro Luis became suddenly and graphically aware of the

dangers that would soon be awaiting any Borja in Rome and barricaded himself with his troops in the Castel Sant'Angelo. The cardinals of the Sacred College responded by taking charge of the Vatican treasury and informing Pedro Luis that the inheritance promised him by his uncle would be withheld until he delivered up the Castel to them. Pedro Luis did this but regretted the decision immediately when he heard that the Orsini family, led by Cardinal Latino Orsini, were riding back into Rome to seek him out and repay, with interest, the attentions he had heaped on them. He was nervously awaiting his impending fate when his brother Rodrigo arrived with a troop of cavalry to escort him out of the city to the Roman port of Ostia, where a boat was to whisk him to the comparative security of Civitavecchia, some miles away along the coast. He was thus saved from the certain retribution of the Orsini, but not from divine intervention. He contracted a fever and died shortly after.

Rodrigo rode back to Rome, haughtily ignoring an angry, seething mob outside the Vatican, to sit at his uncle's bedside. Calixtus, weak, emaciated, and lapsing into periods of unconsciousness, was reaching the end of his time on earth. Rodrigo was holding the frail body in his arms and praying for the old man's soul as Calixtus faded away in the evening of August 6. The memories of that day were to stay with Rodrigo for the rest of his life.

With Calixtus dead, Rodrigo knew the risk he ran every moment he lingered in Rome. But he refused to flee to safety. A funeral was hastily arranged for the dead pope, and Rodrigo joined the small, loyal group which gathered for the interment. Then he turned fearlessly to face the Borja enemies who were hovering like vultures, waiting their moment to strike.

2

RODRIGO BORGIA, PAPAL APPRENTICE.

Courage, personified by the proud bull of the Borja family heraldic device, found a natural resting place on the broad shoulders of Rodrigo. It was an attribute destined to sustain him throughout his life.

The second son of Alonso de Borja's favourite sister, Isabella, and her cousin Jofre de Borja y Doms, Rodrigo was born on New Year's Day, 1431. For the first decade of his life, he and Isabella's five other children lived in reasonable comfort in the family home at Jativa, Catalonia. Jofre de Borja had good connections in the royal court of Aragon, and used them to ensure a good livelihood. A contemporary chronicler wrote, 'He had made many journeys to the benefit of the Spanish Crown, and enjoyed the honour of discharging the greatest offices in that realm. He was a remarkable person of great intelligence, and bearing much responsibility for the affairs of the kingdom, since he had risen to command many fortresses through his watchfulness and high integrity, and those other qualities which vied in his person; having for so long discharged such lofty and conspicuous tasks, he acquired much wealth and credit, and got the reputation, by current report, of being the greatest man of his day.'

Careful attention was given to Rodrigo's early education for, 'when still a child, he revealed the great intelligence he had inherited from his father, indeed the said child attracted respect and esteem because of his disposition and his abilities.' Other skills soon made their presence known: 'Apart from his study of letters he had a great talent for military matters and the handling of arms. From childhood onwards he would go hunting in the countryside with arquebus, pistol, and dagger; and he would likewise display his mettle in this sphere.'

When Rodrigo was just ten years old, his father died. It was a shattering blow which his mother managed to temper by moving her brood into the bishop's palace in Valencia, empty while the incumbent, Alonso de Borja, was absent on royal business in Naples. Rodrigo remained a model student but also developed a vindictive, ferocious streak to his character. The same chronicler relates this horrifying anecdote about the young boy: 'As Rodrigo grew in years, so he also grew in pride and haughtiness, cruelty and tyranny, showing himself stern, implacable, vindictive and unpredictable in his actions. It is said that when only twelve years old, he killed another boy in Valencia – his equal in age, but of low birth – by driving his scabbard again and again into his belly, to punish him for having uttered some indecent words. This was the first test of his pride, and the first incident that forced people to recognize the stuff he was made of, the kind of spirit and temper he had.'

A tradition which lingered through the ages decreed that Rodrigo, as the family's second son, should enter the church. Isabella naturally hoped that Alonso de Borja, close confidant of the king and also the bishop of Valencia, would help her boys. She was not to be disappointed. Uncle Alonso, with no children of his own, took a deep and abiding interest in both Rodrigo and his particular favourite, Pedro Luis, Rodrigo's elder brother. When Alonso became a cardinal, he insisted on paying the fees for the boys to study at the University of Bologna. And it was Alonso's influence with Pope Nicholas V which induced the pontiff to appoint Rodrigo, at the tender age of fourteen, to the Chapter of Valencia, citing his 'probity of life and conduct', and 'laudable proofs of rectitude and virtue'. The local clergy voiced their disagreement in a howl of impotent protest, seeing the family influence at work. Knowing the truth about Rodrigo, the adolescent killer, may have made it impossible for them to believe in the pope's fulsome praise of the boy's life.

Rodrigo was in Rome as a spectator at the ostentatious

wedding of the German Holy Roman Emperor, Frederick III, and Eleanor of Portugal in 1452. He was also an interested bystander during an abortive revolt aimed at establishing a republican government in the city. This was smothered before it came to life by the capture and execution of the conspirators. But of much greater fascination to the full-blooded, impetuous, and stunningly good-looking young man was the hedonistic night life of Rome. Though that city was the seat of the august and infallible leader of the church, it was also the sin capital of Europe. Courtesans flocked there from every corner of Christendom to stake claim to the princes and priests who were wealthy enough to keep them in a manner to which they were only too eager to become accustomed. The matter of priests taking mistresses to ease the frustration of their avowed celibacy was something the church officially frowned upon. In practice, it was just about impossible to find a priest, bishop, or even cardinal who did not keep a concubine or a mistress to visit at intervals. Rodrigo, who had already taken minor church orders, was no exception to the prevailing rule. And the swarthy, lithe, powerfully-built Valencian was a great favourite with the beautiful and enthusiastic ladies of Rome. He developed a legendary reputation as a rampant male, justified by his willingness to bestow his favours generously on the wide variety of females with whom the eternal city tempted him.

His indulgent Uncle Alonso, rare indeed in the church's iniquitous flock in that he avoided women through piety and disinclination, shrugged his shoulders and smiled at Rodrigo's voracious sexual appetite. Secretly, he may have felt somewhat proud of his nephew's success in the tender art of love. It seemed to contribute to the noble and self-assured manner in which the young man deported himself. The questionable morality of a priest behaving as Rodrigo did was something that neither Alonso nor anyone else dwelt upon, for, like most other men who had taken the sacred vows, Rodrigo had not entered the church through conviction or faith. It was a profession, and the church a vehicle to be used to carry him to the upper reaches of society. Such blatant hypocrisy was just another facet of a church battling for temporal survival during the age.

This dissolute way of life matched the unbridled freedom of thought being preached by the brilliant minds who were gathering, notably under the patronage of Pope Nicholas V, in the first flush of the Renaissance's revival of classical arts and learning. The pope's court was generally acknowledged as the most accomplished in Europe. Frescoes by artists such as Benedetto Buonfigli and Bartolomeo di Foligno were appearing in palaces around Rome as Nicholas began the artistic and architectural programme which was to transform the Vatican, culminating in Michelangelo's awe-inspiring creations in the Sistine Chapel half a century later.

Rodrigo was enrolled at a school for relatives of senior Vatican officials and immediately came to the attention of his tutor, Gaspare da Verona. Gaspare's recorded assessment of the young man was: 'He is handsome, with a most cheerful countenance and genial bearing. He is gifted with a honeyed and choice eloquence. Beautiful women are attracted to love him and are excited by him in a quite remarkable way, more powerfully than iron is attracted by a magnet.'

Rodrigo's time was split between Rome and the University of Bologna, where he and his cousin, Luis Juan de Mila, went to study canon law. Pope Nicholas, at Cardinal Alonso de Borja's insistence, saw to it that Rodrigo received his church salaries while his education continued.

The presence of the boys in the papal city of Bologna raised hardly a ripple of interest until their Uncle Alonso was elected as Pope Calixtus. Then it was a very different matter. The cousins attended the enthronement ceremonies in Rome and returned to the university to complete their studies. Rodrigo took up residence amidst the splendour of the Palazzo Gregoriano. Luis Juan, nominated as Governor of the city of Bologna by Calixtus, was installed in splendour at a church palace. Both, not surprisingly, were now highly regarded by their tutors and passed their final examinations with distinction.

27

When Calixtus's death left Rodrigo vulnerable with the Borja enemies thirsting for his blood, he turned to face the first great crisis of his life. If he doubted the danger, it was indelibly confirmed for him by the mob which rampaged across Rome, looting his palace as they cut a swath of destruction through the Spanish quarter. He was the only member of his family brave or foolish enough to remain in the turbulent city. His courage was to be rewarded when he succeeded not only in staying alive, but also in retaining a firm grip on his position of authority. He may not have been his uncle's favourite, but he was certainly a man favoured by fortune.

Still only twenty-seven years old, his ambition was matched by his confidence. Despite his youth, he stood head and shoulders above his contemporaries in the maelstrom of power which was Rome. His courage, skill, and resolution ensured that the future belonged to him.

He was a dominating presence in the conclave of cardinals called to elect a successor to his uncle. The first candidate to lead the field was wealthy French Cardinal Guillaume d'Estouteville, who blatantly tried to buy the papacy with extravagant promises to any of his colleagues promising support. Another leading contender, Cardinal Aeneas Sylvius Piccolomini from Siena, asked Rodrigo, a close friend, if he had sold his vote to the Frenchman. Rodrigo confessed that he had because he felt d'Estouteville was certain to win, and there seemed no point in falling out of favour with the new pope. 'I am looking out for my own interest', he acknowledged. 'I shall not lose the Vice-Chancellorship. I have a note assuring me of that. If I do not vote for him, the others will elect him anyway, and I shall be stripped of my office.' Piccolomini told Rodrigo that the Vice-Chancellorship had also been promised to one of the other French cardinals in exchange for his vote, and that d'Estouteville was more likely to honour a pledge to a fellow countryman.

Rodrigo voted for d'Estouteville anyway but, fortunately for him, the Frenchman failed to win the necessary two-thirds' majority. When Piccolomini pledged to retain Rodrigo as his Vice-Chancellor, the charismatic young cardinal stood to acclaim his friend: 'I accede to the Cardinal of Siena!' The waverers in the Sacred College followed his decisive lead, Piccolomini was elected as Pope Pius II, and he gratefully confirmed Rodrigo as Vice-Chancellor. Pius was fully aware of Rodrigo's value to the papacy. He confided to a journal: 'Our Chancellor is young, it is true, but his conduct and good sense make him seem older than his years; in wisdom he is equal to his uncle.' Up above Rodrigo's head, his guardian angel's wings must have been beating steadily.

Rodrigo, who now prudently adopted the Italian spelling of his family name (Borgia), was a vastly different man to his uncle, the austere and pious Calixtus. He revelled in the ostentatious glamour of the times, the splendid and ornate homes, the flood of magnificent works of art which was filling the churches and palaces. Rewarded generously by Calixtus for loyal service to the family cause, Rodrigo became an extremely wealthy man from his church incomes, and was regarded as the richest of the cardinals, with the possible exception of d'Estouteville. A contemporary, dazzled by Rodrigo's prodigious wealth, recorded, 'His papal offices, his numerous abbeys in Italy and Spain, and his three bishoprics of Valencia, Porto and Cartagena, yield him a vast income, and it is said that the office of Vice-Chancellor alone brings him in eight thousand gold florins. His plate, his pearls, his stuffs embroidered with silk and gold, and his books in every department of learning are very numerous, and all are of a magnificence worthy of a king or a pope. I need not mention the innumerable bed-hangings, the trappings for his horses, nor his magnificent wardrobe, nor the vast amount of gold coin in his possession.'

He did, however, need all the money he could get, for he squandered his fortune in true Renaissance style. He joined the burgeoning multitude of *nouveau riche* sponsors who vied with each other to obtain the services of the painters, sculptors, architects, poets and scientists whose skills were heralding the rebirth of the beauties of an all but forgotten classical

29

age. Rodrigo showered money on painters and sculptors to encourage them to produce works for him. The resultant creations he either placed in his home or donated to churches in and around Rome. But his greatest contribution to the golden age of the Renaissance was his spectacular palace, built on the site of a defunct mint which he had bought from Calixtus.

All who saw the building agreed that it overshadowed the other magnificent townhouses of Rome. Rodrigo personally supervised the building of the palace, which employed the skills of a team of the world's finest craftsmen for several years. The splendour of its design revealed him as a supreme arbiter of style and taste. It was constructed around a galleried courtyard, and its seemingly endless rooms featured exquisite tapestries, furnishings, and displays of gold and silver plate which left visitors gasping in amazement. A vivid description of Rodrigo's home, set just across the River Tiber from the Vatican, has been bequeathed to us by the Milanese Cardinal Ascanio Sforza who wrote, 'The palace is splendidly decorated; the walls of the great entrance hall are hung with tapestries depicting various historical scenes. A small drawing room leads off this, which was also decorated with fine tapestries; the carpets on the floor harmonized with the furnishings which included a sumptuous day bed upholstered in red satin with a canopy over it, and a chest on which was laid out a vast and beautiful collection of gold and silver plate. Beyond this there were two more rooms, one hung with fine satin, carpeted, and with another canopied bed covered with Alexandrine velvet; the other even more ornate with a couch covered in cloth of gold. In this room the central table was covered with a cloth of Alexandrine velvet and surrounded by finely carved chairs.'

The citizens of Rome watched the palace grow to daunting architectural proportions which dominated its area of the city. Pius II compared it to the Golden House of Nero. No expense was spared in the building and furnishing of the palace and from the imposing tower built into the facade, Rodrigo could look down at the resplendent, but demonstrably more modest, homes of his fellow cardinals. The courtyard, with its Tuscan columns, still stands today as the central core of the Palazzo Sforza-Cesarini.

Rodrigo's reputation grew with his increasingly lavish banquets for hordes of guests. He did everything possible to impress with sumptuous meals served up on giant gold platters held aloft by page-boys while minstrels played soothing background music. So theatrically spectacular were his presentations that successive popes insisted on utilizing his services as official court entertainer.

A passion for show was an outstanding feature of Rodrigo's personality. He loved entertaining on the grand scale, but he also had a very fundamental reason for making an impression on his world. The dimensions and style of his palatial life were designed to demonstrate his power, both to the ordinary people of Rome, to his colleagues and rivals in the church, and to the princes from all over Europe who came to sample his legendary hospitality. This gave him an aura of psychological dominance which had a telling effect on those it reached out to embrace. His objective, carefully concealed for many years of his cardinalate, was the papacy. He had a shrewd understanding of men, particularly those associated with the church, and realized that his showmanship would impress on them his ability to stand aloof and above the masses – in short, that he was worthy to accede to the throne of St. Peter.

His wholehearted sponsorship of Renaissance ideals led him to finance the search for ancient manuscripts. He also backed the revival of the classical theatre and collected some of the earliest printed books from the hand-presses of early printers such as Schweinheim and Ponnartz. Writers and scholars were regular and esteemed guests at his home, as Rodrigo sought to gain by basking in their reflected glory, and he made a firm friend of Lorenz Bahaim, a celebrated German scholar and historian. He lavished funds on country palaces and castles, restoring them to unprecedented glory on the lines of classical antiquity. In 1460 he took a summer holiday with Pius II in Corsignano, and decided on a whim to have a splendid palace built there for himself.

From Spain he brought with him two great passions. The first was for the aristocratic pastime of hunting, and he became a familiar sight charging across the countryside dressed in cloak and boots. His stables were filled with the finest horses available and he bred a pack of hunting dogs of which he was fiercely proud. His second burning passion was for bullfights, and he staged many, to the delight or dismay of his new Italian friends.

Such self-indulgence was made possible by the consummate skill with which he exercised his power as Vice-Chancellor behind the papal throne. He was always at the pope's side in public ceremonies, a puppet-master surreptitiously operating the strings. Responsible for the day-to-day government of papal affairs, he was also President of the Sacred Rota, the supreme court to the church. He held these august posts under five different pontiffs, who all came to rely on him absolutely. This reliance he used assiduously to consolidate his power and wealth, largely through collecting various church positions and the resultant salaries. Lesser church posts which he did not care to hold himself he auctioned off to the highest bidder. He was brilliant, decisive, devious, and an electrifying opportunist who was also capable of patiently seeing long-term plans through to their conclusion, as he strode confidently and boldly along the corridors of power. These diverse abilities saw him securely and successfully through the years of makeshift alliances of convenience. They also earned him the fulsome praise of the Florentine statesman Niccolo Machiavelli, whose name added a new and formidable word to the vocabulary of intrigue. As he detailed in his book, *The Prince*, Machiavelli regarded Rodrigo Borgia's life as a textbook on the ruthless but brilliantly efficient exercise of power.

Rodrigo exhibited his Renaissance character in his love of art, of architecture – and of women. Shortly after acceding to the papacy, Pius II took his court for a sojourn in the cooler climes of Lombardy, in the north of Italy. But life in that stifling provincial atmosphere proved too dull for the energetic Rodrigo, who entertained himself by seducing the stunning wife of a notably dim-witted nobleman. Her name has been lost in the swirling mists of history which shroud so much of this era, but the lady in question clearly found the presence of the virile and exotic young cardinal irresistible.

Though he managed to keep word of this escapade from Pius, Rodrigo was not so fortunate when he took advantage of his position to indulge himself with a group of ladies in Siena. The occasion was a baptismal feast to which Rodrigo and Cardinal d'Estouteville had been invited as honoured guests. After the church ceremony, a party was held in the grounds of a sumptuous Siena home. Then, for five hours in the evening, the two cardinals retired to a walled and secluded garden with their entourage and the female guests of the gathering. All others, and especially the men of Siena, were expressly excluded from the garden. Soon all Siena was gossiping about the incident. It snowballed into a great scandal and the story reached the ears of an astounded and outraged Pope Pius. He immediately took it upon himself to reprimand his Vice-Chancellor for demeaning his elevated position.

In a scorching letter, Pius wrote to Rodrigo: 'Beloved Son, We have learned that Your Worthiness, forgetful of the high office with which you are invested, was present from the seventeenth to the twenty second hour, four days ago, in the gardens of Giovanni de Bichis, where there were several women of Siena, women wholly given over to worldly vanities. Your companion was one of your colleagues whom his years, if not the dignity of his office, ought to have reminded of his duty. We have heard that the dance was indulged in in all wantonness; none of the allurements of love were lacking, and you conducted yourself in a wholly worldly manner. Shame forbids the mention of all that took place, for not only the things themselves but their very names are unworthy of your rank. In order that your lust might be all the more unrestrained, the husbands, fathers, brothers, and kinsmen of the young women and girls were not invited to be present. You and a few servants were the leaders and inspirers of this orgy. It is said that nothing is now talked of in Siena but your vanity, which is the subject of general ridicule.' After chastizing Rodrigo for 'behaving as if you were one of a group of young laymen', Pius pointed out that his conduct reflected badly on the already much maligned church clergy, who were obliged to contend with a great many slurs, both warranted and unwarranted. He concluded that the incident was a scar on the memory of Pope Calixtus, 'who, in many people's judgement, did ill to load you with such honours.'

Pius seems to have sent this letter off in the heat of sudden anger, for he later sent a second, more considered, rebuke. He agreed that he had probably been too hasty in believing all he was told, but still implored Rodrigo to keep away from such gatherings and 'to take care of your honour with greater prudence'.

Rodrigo, chastened, promised that he would lead a more circumspect life. In fact, the reprimands did nothing to curb his appetite for the pursuit and conquest of women. The hot-blooded and passionate Rodrigo had an unbounded zest for life which made it impossible for him to say no. But they did make him more prudent about his amorous exploits, while in private he remained as promiscuous and outrageous as ever. However, after the Siena incident he took care to avoid any display which might be regarded as a blatant disregard for ecclesiastical conventions.

During the papacy of Pius II, Rodrigo fathered two children, but he made sure the pontiff heard nothing about them. The first was born in 1462 and named Pedro Luis, after Rodrigo's brother, who had died after his dramatic escape from Rome. The second, Isabella, entered the world in 1467. Both were borne by the same mother, but so securely did Rodrigo draw the veil of secrecy over this part of his existence that her name, and indeed anything which might help to identify her, has been lost. We can only be certain that she possessed the dazzling beauty which the proud and demanding Rodrigo insisted on in women. The children were, of course, illegitimate, but no great distinction was made about this at that time. Secretive though he may have been about his children, Rodrigo made sure they were brought up and educated in suitable style. Pedro Luis was dispatched at a tender age to Spain, where indulgent relatives nursed him through adolescence. Isabella was brought up in Rome, but at a prudent distance from the Vatican and any prospective scandal. Rodrigo liked his children, and gloried in the joy of their open and innocent minds, but he did not let them jeopardize his ambitions.

Pope Pius's opinions on Rodrigo's elastic morals must have been tempered by the fact that in his younger days, Pius had also been something of a lady's man. He was also aware of the value of Rodrigo's abilities as an administrator, and made sure that the Vice-Chancellor's power remained undiminished. To underline his faith in Rodrigo, Pius ordained that he be made Bishop of Cartagena, a post which added considerably to the cardinal's already large prestige and wealth.

Thus, Rodrigo's power base grew inexorably stronger, and, as the years passed, so the pope's reliance on his wisdom and judgement increased. An assessment of Rodrigo comes from a letter of the period, which describes him as 'a man of versatile intellect, and great sense of imagination; an eloquent speaker and well-read in a rather general way; he has a warm nature but above all is brilliantly skilled in conducting affairs. He is immensely wealthy and in great favour with many kings and princes.'

Pope Pius, following the lead of Calixtus, became obsessed with the dream of wresting the Holy Land from the Moslem Turks. Like so many other popes, he hoped to have his name carved deep in the stone tablets of Christian history. His first attempt was in the form of a letter which he sent to the Turkish sultan, suggesting that the ruler should surrender his lands to papal authority, and accept a church crown. This was naïvety to the point of absurdity. He was clearly drifting away from the safe anchorage of reality.

Pius came to devote all his energies to the planning of a crusade, while Rodrigo did all he could behind the scenes at the Vatican to minimize the damage caused to the church by the astronomical costs of such an enterprise. But he also wanted to minimize the damage to himself. When the pope talked of creating a large number of new jobs in the Vatican Chancellory to sell off in order to raise funds for the crusade, Rodrigo vetoed the scheme because he felt it would tend to undermine his personal authority.

The Christian kings of Europe did not share Pius's zeal for the holy war, so the pope announced that he would personally lead the crusading warriors. It was an idea rich in madness. For Pius was old, debilitated by illness, and had no experience of leading troops in battle. Rodrigo was as aware as anyone else of the craziness of the pope's religious fervour. In fact, he was none too eager to join what he saw as a suicidal mission. But he was vividly aware that the reward for disloyalty came as speedily as that for loyalty, so he went along with Pius merely to keep his position in ecclesiastical life secure. A confirmed sycophant when necessary, he told Pius, 'I will be at your side on sea and on land, and even, if necessary, will follow you through fire.' So eager was he to demonstrate his support for the pope's dream that he fitted out a galley for the crusading fleet at his own expense – the only cardinal to do so.

In 1464 he gloomily accompanied the fervent but ailing Pius to Ancona, the Adriatic port from which the crusade was to be launched. They lingered too long in the city which was appallingly overcrowded with reluctant and poorly equipped crusaders. In the cramped and unsanitary conditions, the plague broke out. Rodrigo, conscious of a rising panic, considered deserting the pope and his insane venture. But Fate intervened to make the decision for him when the frail and sickly pope suddenly died.

Rodrigo was far from the only person to breathe a sigh of relief as the gathered soldiers of Christ broke camp. He and the other cardinals who had felt constrained to follow the pope scurried back to Rome, where Pius II was quickly consigned to the earth. Then they formed a conclave to elect a new pontiff. Rodrigo, who had gone down with fever

36

in Ancona, was not well enough to play an active role in the political infighting which accompanied the election. He was obliged to watch passively from the sidelines as his old friend and ally Pietro Barbo, the cardinal from Venice, became Pope Paul II. Luck was once again firmly on his side.

A brief power battle followed immediately, for the Sacred College, ever hungry for real power of its own, had contrived what it believed to be a foolproof method of obtaining this. Before the conclave, each member had agreed to the setting up of an Ecumenical Council with powers of veto over church legislation, and signed a document to that effect. The new pope, though not considered very intelligent – he had, for example, never mastered Latin – promptly reneged on the agreement and started imposing his will in the most assertive way. The Ecumenical Council was consigned to oblivion, and the cardinals, who had elected him as Christ's infallible representative on earth, were powerless to oppose him. But one complained in a letter, 'The man is beginning to put on high and mighty airs, and to puff himself up in his own esteem.' Pope Paul confirmed this view when he ordered for himself an incredible pearl-studded tiara and a fabulous ceremonial chair, which cost more than some of the ornamental palaces of Rome.

In the face of such disgruntled opposition from the cardinals, Paul II leaned on Rodrigo Borgia even more than his predecessor had. Though still only thirty-three, Rodrigo was the senior cardinal and should have placed the papal tiara on the new pontiff's head in the coronation ceremony, held on a specially constructed dais in front of St Peter's. However, still affected by fever, he had been unable to attend. This absence was noted, and a falling from favour was suspected. But he was not only confirmed as Vice-Chancellor, he was also allowed by Pope Paul to take control of church affairs in a quite unprecedented manner. His wealth and influence expanded accordingly.

Paul II was a thoroughly typical Renaissance pope. Frivolous and worldly, he spent lavishly on the arts. From an aristocratic Venetian family, he heightened the splendour of the Vatican and injected a new and vibrant gaiety into the Roman carnival season. He also vigorously enforced papal power in the Romagna, with Rodrigo's able and enthusiastic assistance. The ruling families, notably the Orsini, were called very firmly into line.

During the first months of Pope Paul's reign, Rome was smitten with earthquakes, hurricanes and pestilence and Rodrigo Borgia's palace was hit by a thunderbolt. Enemies attributed all this to a sort of divine retribution. When apoplexy, brought on by sunstroke, claimed the life of Pope Paul in the high summer of 1471, Rodrigo strode into the cardinal's conclave as if he were the man of the moment. In fact, he was still considered too young to be pope. So instead he used his prodigious influence to engineer the selection of Cardinal Francesco della Rovere as Pope Sixtus IV.

The new pope had been Minister-General of the Franciscan order of monks, and was a man of unblemished reputation. His election was viewed as a reaction against the materialistic Paul II. This, however, did not deter Sixtus from rewarding Rodrigo with another valuable, and unearned church income.

Sixtus had in fact succumbed to the metamorphosis which seemed an inevitable result of exchanging the purple robes of a cardinal for the shoes of the fisherman. A learned, respected theologian and monastic figure, the follower of Our Lady of Poverty astounded everyone by the ease with which he adapted to the authoritarian papal rule. He exercised nepotism on a greater scale than even the dedicated practitioner Calixtus. A string of his nephews were appointed cardinals as he strove to construct a dynastic foundation in the Vatican. Outstanding among them was the restless, energetic and precociously talented Giuliano della Rovere, who shed his Franciscan robe to reveal a fine athletic figure and a nimble brain. At twenty-eight, he was clearly a man for the future. A kindred spirit to Rodrigo, the two men quickly became firm friends and cohorts.

That same year the mysterious lady who bore Rodrigo's

first two children presented him with another daughter, Girolama. Once again, the cloak of anonymity prevented news of the event from reaching either the new pontiff or his colleagues in the Sacred College.

The next year, Rodrigo was one of five cardinals appointed as Papal Legates Extraordinary and dispatched to various parts of Europe to drum up support for a crusade which Sixtus hoped to mount. Rodrigo was the natural candidate to be sent to Spain, his homeland, where the mission had a vital secondary purpose. Ferdinand, the seventeen-year-old son and heir of John II, King of Aragon, had secretly married his cousin Isabella, sister of Castile's King Henry IV. The dynastic union held out the tempting promise of an end to the consistent internal wars which were tearing Spain apart, and perhaps, as a result, energy to spare for a crusade. But, because of the close family link between the teenage couple a papal dispensation was needed to legalize the marriage in the eyes of the church.

Accompanied by a delegation which would have honoured a reigning monarch, Rodrigo left Rome in traditional style escorted through the Porta San Paolo by all the other cardinals in May 1472. Included in his entourage to Spain were three bishops and, a concession to the tenor of the age, two painters, Paolo di San Leocadio da Reggio and Francesco Pagano. They sailed in two Neapolitan ships from Ostia to Valencia where Rodrigo had spent his youth, and they made a spectacular entry which is described in a contemporary letter : 'All the councilmen, the governor general, and other prominent noblemen and gentlemen, to the number of twelve, waited for him with a magnificent canopy, under which the cardinal entered, mounted on his steed; and the porters of the canopy were all on foot. And when they arrived at the city walls, where the gates were overhung with crimson draperies, he entered the city to the various sounds of trumpets and kettledrums.'

The city's noblemen vied with each other for the privilege of holding the canopy over his head to protect him from the fierce Mediterranean sun and almost the whole city turned out onto the streets to watch his state reception and procession to Valencia Cathedral, where he celebrated mass. This was a particularly nostalgic moment for Rodrigo, who had prayed in the cathedral as a boy. Still Bishop of Valencia, though he had not set foot there in decades, a lavish banquet attended by every civic dignitary was given in his honour. Rodrigo sailed through the proceedings with a majestic, charismatic air which impressed all who saw him. He extended his stay in Valencia to make a series of diocesan visits, a rare treat for his unshepherded bishopric.

Then Rodrigo headed north to Lerida, where he met with King John and the youthful Ferdinand. He was impressed by Ferdinand, and it did not take him long to decide on the wisdom of church sanction for the marriage. Sixtus had given him full authority to decide the issue, and Rodrigo carried with him a signed but undated Papal Bull which declared the legality of the match. He filled in the missing details on the document, placing the official seal of approval on the union, for a jubilant King John. The marriage was to have an enormous political significance, for it welded together two rival states and laid the foundation for an eventual union of the whole of Spain. It also bonded together the couple who were bold enough some twenty years later to finance an apparently crazy transoceanic expedition by a Genoese explorer, Christopher Columbus.

After a pleasant sojourn hosted by the grateful Aragon court, Rodrigo moved on to Castile, where he ran into opposition to the sanction of the marriage from Archbishop Gonzalez de Mendoza. However, Rodrigo had expected this and was prepared to meet the challenge. He had advised Pope Sixtus that he believed the archbishop could be bribed with the promise of a cardinalate, and at his meeting with de Mendoza, Rodrigo produced a papal letter offering just that. Miraculously, de Mendoza's reservations disappeared, and the archbishop saw to it that King Henry and the rest of his court expressed heartfelt support for the marriage.

It was a significant triumph for Rodrigo, and marked the beginning of his career as a roving master diplomat for Pope

Sixtus. On a personal level, it assured Rodrigo of the loyalty of the Spanish kings and forged a friendship with Ferdinand which was to survive for over twenty years.

The Castile court fêted Rodrigo through Christmas of 1472, and he later returned to Aragon, where he made a tour of his Spanish estates and proudly showed off his Jativa birthplace to his travelling companions. Though malicious gossip about Rodrigo's immoral behaviour at both royal courts filtered back to Pope Sixtus, he studiously ignored it on the grounds that it was probably inspired by jealousy and that, in any event, Rodrigo was too valuable to the papal interest for anything to be done about the gossip.

A group of young and hopeful Valencians who wanted to try their luck in Rome joined Rodrigo when he left Spain for the last time in his life in September, 1473. The two Venetian galleys carrying them ran into a violent storm off the Tuscany coast. One sank outright and most of the young Valencians drowned. The other, carrying the fortuitous Vice-Chancellor, managed to beach in the mouth of the River Arno near Pisa. The survivors were cared for by the Florentine ruler, Lorenzo de'Medici (known as 'The Magnificent') until they were recovered enough to complete their journey to Rome overland.

Shortly after the successful conclusion of his Spanish mission, Rodrigo Borgia met Vannozza de' Cattanei, the exotic woman with whom he had a long affair. He was in his early forties; she was thirty-two. Vannozza's origins are relatively obscure. We know she was born in 1442, in an Italian country village. Her father, the painter Jacopo Pinctoria, and her mother Donna Menica migrated with their daughter to Rome, which held out prospects of work for indigent craftsmen. Possibly Rodrigo met Vannozza when he visited her father's workshop. He certainly fell deeply in love with her. She was strikingly beautiful, with an oval face, almond eyes, and a small, well-shaped mouth. Most women of her day were firmly locked in matrimony before the age of twenty but it seems likely that her impoverished father could not afford a dowry to lure a prospective husband, which would mean she had no chance of a conventional marriage. Rodrigo could not wed her, of course, because of his vow of celibacy, but this did not prevent him installing his new mistress in a fine house which was conveniently close to his palace, while being distant enough for discretion. The mores of the time made no great distinction between a wife and a concubine, so her family did not feel disgraced. Conversely, because the Vice-Chancellor was, after all, the most important man in the church after the pope, it was construed as something of an honour.

His liaison with Vannozza was an open secret among the Vatican circle, but Rodrigo still felt a pressing need for circumspection. He vividly recalled Pope Pius's admonition that he should keep his private life well hidden. So he decided that Vannozza should have a husband to give her a cloak of respectability. Rodrigo selected a suitably pliable candidate in Domenico da Rignano, an elderly lawyer. The marriage was celebrated in 1474, and Rodrigo gave the couple a town house close to his home as a wedding gift. He also provided the dowry which Vannozza's father had not been able to afford. Then he made sure that Signor Rignano's work kept him travelling, to clear the way for his own clandestine visits.

Vannozza was a woman of mercurial temperament, a vivid contrast to the smouldering Rodrigo. She captured his affections, cured his appetite for other women, and held on to him for some years. She was the only woman with whom he ever had a lasting relationship and he cared for their four children with a depth of emotion denied to the first three.

While most Romans wilted under the ferocious summer sun, and the plague threatened the city, Rodrigo and Vannozza sought refuge in one of his many castles in the cooler mountainous countryside. Their first child, a son called Cesare, was born during just such a sojourn in 1475. The couple were ecstatic about the birth, but Cesare was passed off as the legal offspring of her husband, the absent Signor da Rignano. When this husband of convenience died, Rodrigo recruited a Vatican secretary, Giorgio San Croce, as his replacement. Like his predecessor, Giorgio was dispatched far and wide on church business, while providing the perfect smokescreen for Rodrigo and Vannozza's next two children. A son, Juan, was born in 1476, followed by a daughter, Lucrezia, in 1480. Rodrigo adored Lucrezia, and made no attempt to hide his feelings. The fourth and last of their children, another son, Jofre, was born in 1481.

The children, naturally, could not be brought up under Rodrigo's roof, but they spent their early childhood as a solid family unit, their lives very much dominated by their father. Rodrigo spent a lot of time with them, and he saw to it that the best education was made available for the two elder boys, Cesare and Juan. They shared the same tutor, and were taught Latin, Spanish, Italian, French and Greek. They read the classical authors and learned music, drawing, arithmetic and geometry.

Rodrigo paid careful attention to planning the course of his children's lives. His eldest son, Pedro Luis, still studying in Spain, was marked out for a military career, while the two sisters, Isabella and Girolama, were to be found suitable husbands. Pietro Matuzzi, a Roman nobleman who held an important job in the city administration, was selected as Isabella's husband, and Rodrigo gave the couple a town house close to his own palace. Girolama was married to Gianandrea Cesarini, a member of a wealthy and illustrious Roman family, in a very stylish wedding which was a major social event. However, both the newlyweds were dead within months, claimed by one of the feverish diseases which perennially cast their sinister menace over the cramped and sweltering city.

Cesare, as Rodrigo's second son, was destined for a career in the church, but first there was an obstacle to be circumvented, and in 1480, when the boy was five years old, Pope Sixtus issued a Papal Bull which declared Cesare legitimate to the point where he was eligible for all ecclesiastical offices except a cardinalate. The Vatican paperwork for this declaration was prepared by none other than Rodrigo Borgia. Two years later, Cesare was made an Apostolic Protonotary by Sixtus. In the same year, Rodrigo persuaded his friend,

Ferdinand of Aragon, to declare that the inferiority status of Cesare's illegitimacy was ended. This opened the way for the boy to hold lordships in Aragon, and to be appointed to church positions within that realm. Rodrigo was then able to engineer, in rapid succession, Cesare's appointments as Canon of Valencia Cathedral, still in the Vice-Chancellor's diocese, Archdeacon of Jativa, the family's home town, Rector of Gandia, Provost and Treasurer of Cartagena Cathedral in another of Rodrigo's dioceses, Archdeacon of Tarragona Cathedral, and Canon of the collegiate church in the royal city of Lerida. Cesare was, of course, far too young to fulfil the duties of these offices, but nevertheless he was paid the salaries. The money was used by Rodrigo to pay for his sons' expensive, privately-tutored education. Pedro Luis, eldest of Rodrigo's first brood of children, was subjected to a similar papal whitewash in 1483, when he was also declared legitimate by Sixtus and served in the army of Ferdinand of Aragon.

When Rodrigo had returned to Rome from Spain, he found that church politics had altered slightly. Rome, which was being rebuilt into a capital of elegance and emerging as a centre of diplomatic intrigue, had become something of a Rovere family fief. Sixtus had imported numerous relatives to take over key church posts. But there was no question of the ever-valuable and always resourceful Vice-Chancellor being jettisoned. Rodrigo settled easily into the new order of things, continuing to confirm his control over his lands and fortress within the Papal States. Sixtus certainly appreciated Rodrigo's wisdom and the ordinary people of Rome, who knew nothing of his licentious private life, revered the Vice-Chancellor. When he rode by in gilded and berobed splendour, they would kneel in the gutters to pay their homage.

Rodrigo was chosen as the Papal Legate to the Neapolitan court to officiate at the wedding of Ferdinand of Aragon's sister, Queen Juana of Naples. Sixtus sought a close friendship with Naples because he hoped to make that state an ally for a conquering war he schemed against Florence. Rodrigo was eager for the same link, but with a different motivation.

The Turks were rampaging through the Balkans, almost within cannonball range of Italy, and he realized that a solid alliance of the Italian states might be necessary for survival. Rodrigo managed to divert Sixtus from his planned war against Florence, and the Turkish threat died in 1480 with the demise of Sultan Mohammed II, for the ruler's two sons first squabbled then went to war over the succession. It was a stroke of luck which saved Europe from almost certain subjugation.

The death of Pope Sixtus in August 1484 precipitated a power struggle between the two cardinals who emerged as the men most likely to succeed him – Rodrigo Borgia and Giuliano della Rovere, Sixtus's energetic and able nephew. The Roman street mob also hurled itself into the fray, as they did whenever a pope died. Looters roared through the Vatican apartments, taking with them everthing moveable as they stripped the rooms like a swarm of locusts. Rodrigo and the other cardinals barricaded themselves in their palaces until the tumult subsided. Then they emerged to hammer out the deals and agreements for the coming conclave.

Rodrigo believed that, at last, his hour was at hand. He threw aside the cloak of humility which he had used to present himself as an obedient servant of the church, and mounted a vigorous campaign to secure the ultimate prize – the papacy. Everything he owned was put on offer to win the necessary Sacred College votes: his present office of Vice-Chancellor, his palace with its priceless furnishings, his myriad church offices, all his salaries, the cash he had accumulated over the years. A man who fervently believed that everyone had a price, Rodrigo knew he had most to offer, and therefore did not see how he could lose.

But he did. And, to a large extent, it was the power he had wielded behind the scenes for so long which counted against him. For his fellow cardinals feared him. This, combined with powerful backing for della Rovere, at forty-one a young, vital and potent force, proved too much. As the first vote was taken in the conclave, it was clear that their rival challenges would neutralize each other. So they joined forces to ensure the election of a compromise candidate who, they hoped, would serve both their interests. Their opportunistic choice fell upon the timorous cardinal from Genoa, Battista Cibo. They dragged him from obscurity, had him proclaimed Pope Innocent VIII, and used him as a puppet.

Rodrigo was by now aged fifty-three, and realized he could not afford to leave matters to chance any longer. He immediately started laying plans for the next election. Pope Innocent retained him as Vice-Chancellor, and Rodrigo used the position to gather allies all over Italy, and set about patching up the family quarrel with the still-powerful Colonna and Orsini clans. With an assiduous distribution of favours, he used Innocent's reign to consolidate his position for an invincible assault. His ostentatious living and entertaining were all part of his plan to present himself as the most powerful of men, and the prime choice as heir apparent.

Pope Innocent proved to be insipid, harmless, and friendly to all. But his worldliness, demonstrated by the sons he had sired during his youth, was confirmed when he spent the eve of his election purchasing the necessary votes with signed promises of rewards. At his side, almost guiding the pen, was the figure of Giuliano della Rovere, who was to remain a shadowy influence throughout Innocent's reign. The ambitious cardinal so dominated his titular boss that a Florentine envoy wrote to Lorenzo de' Medici, 'Send a good letter to the Cardinal of San Pietro (della Rovere) for he is pope more than the pope.' Della Rovere, already City Prefect of Rome by order of his uncle, was also made Captain-General of the Church, which gave him command of the church army. As della Rovere's influence and power expanded, so Rodrigo's antipathy towards his rival grew. His feelings were reciprocated, and the antagonism between the two men remained a feature of their existence for the rest of Rodrigo's life.

With a weak and pliable pontiff at the helm, corruption blossomed in the Vatican. Church offices were blatantly auctioned off to the highest bidders by Innocent, and, for a price, a group in the Curia would forge Papal Bulls granting dispensations. One observer wrote, 'Our churches, priests, altars, sacred rites, our prayers, our heavens, our very God are purchasable.' Innocent crowned his efforts when his son Franceschetto, a notorious gambler, debaucher and degenerate, was married in a Vatican chapel to Maddalena de' Medici, young daughter of Lorenzo de' Medici, the Florentine ruler. In exchange, Innocent made Lorenzo's thirteen-year-old son, Giovanni, a cardinal. This astounded even the confirmed hypocrites of the papal court, so Lorenzo sought to calm them by claiming his son was two years older.

Rodrigo at this point started easing Vannozza de' Cattanei out of his life. In part, this was because he believed his well-known association with her was inconsistent with his papal ambitions. It was also to make room for a certain radiantly beautiful young girl who had caught his eye. But he did not completely end his relationship with Vannozza: he looked after her financially for years, and when her second husband, Signor San Croce, died, he found another suitable spouse and paid her dowry for the third time. This latest bridegroom was Carlo Canale, a man who had served as secretary to his fellow Spanish cardinal, Gonzaga. They were married in 1486, and the wedding was solemnized in the presence of Rodrigo's lawyer. A job for Vannozza's new husband was created in the Vatican where the Vice-Chancellor could keep an eye on him. Signor Canale was in no way put out to be used in this way by Rodrigo Borgia, though he was aware of exactly what was going on. On the contrary, he was most grateful for the connection with the Borgias, and the inherent power which his new station in life gave him. Vannozza also had many reasons to feel content about her relationship with Rodrigo. With the money he had given her, she became an independent woman of property.

The young girl who had captured Rodrigo's attention was Giulia Farnese. Though still a teenager, Giulia had a certain delicate porcelain elegance and was already a legendary beauty whom the Romans referred to as Giulia la Bella. They met when Rodrigo, who wanted to keep control of his children, had Lucrezia and Jofre moved into the nearby palace of Monte Giordano, where his widowed cousin, Adriana del Mila, became their governess. Adriana had been married to an Orsini, Ludovico, Lord of Bassanello – a match arranged by Rodrigo – and she had a young son, Orsino Orsini, who was betrothed to Giulia. Rodrigo was smitten by her on sight and she, in turn, was completely overawed by the berobed presence of the church's Vice-Chancellor. The modesty and trembling fear Giulia displayed only served to provoke his desire, and they soon became lovers. Meanwhile, her betrothal flowered into a marriage in 1489. Since the fathers of the couple were both dead, Rodrigo made his palace available for the magnificent ceremony, and he was a cynically pious spectator and witness signatory as his nineteen-year-old mistress was joined in matrimony to the gawky, thirteen-year-old boy. Adriana del Mila, who felt responsible for the young girl, knew exactly what was going on, but was unable to influence events. Though strong-willed, imperious and highly intelligent she was no match for the wily Rodrigo. He knew he was on secure ground with his cousin, who was fiercely devoted to him and (a major reason for her selection as governess) a fellow Catalan. Rodrigo made Giulia's bridegroom a wedding gift of a *condotta*, a freelance military commission, in the service of an Italian lord, and the couple moved into a suite of rooms in Adriana del Mila's palatial home. The young man's army duties kept him conveniently away from his bride for much of the time. The Vice-Chancellor was a regular visitor to Monte Giordano, ostensibly to visit his cousin, but in fact to luxuriate in the company of his beautiful young mistress. Lucrezia, for her part, loved Giulia as a much-admired older sister.

Soon all of Roman society was aflame with gossip about the affair. The men spoke with sympathy of the cuckolded husband and angrily of Rodrigo despoiling the image of the church by flaunting his mistress. But they were mostly expressing jealousy at seeing a man who, at nearly sixty, was able to capture the affections of a lovely young girl.

Giulia Farnese was Rodrigo's last lover. Their relationship was wild and passionate, interspersed with the apparently conflicting emotions of tenderness and jealousy. For Giulia, the affair represented the most momentous years of her life. The liaison set her mediocre family on course for undreamt-of fame and fortune, and reached culmination half a century later when Giulia's brother Alexander became pope.

Rodrigo's other abiding passion was for his children. He still felt his Spanish roots strongly: most of his entourage were Spaniards, so he saw to it that his children had Spanish tutors. His first language was Catalan and most of his correspondence was written in either Catalan or Castilian. As a natural consequence, his children always felt more comfortable speaking in Spanish dialects than Italian.

Rodrigo's solid Spanish links were bonded even more strongly by the excellent service his son, Pedro Luis, gave as an officer in the army of Ferdinand, by now King of Aragon. This amity was shaken, however, when in 1484 Rodrigo claimed the Bishopric of Seville for himself, and added it to his seemingly interminable list of church appointments. Ferdinand had thought the position would be a suitable sinecure for his illegitimate son Alfonso, and was furious at what he regarded as a usurpation. He had already been enraged by Rodrigo's high-handed manner of gathering church benefices in Aragon, when he seemed to disregard royal authority.

This last show of arrogance led Ferdinand to seek retribution against the Borgias by ordering the imprisonment of Pedro Luis, who was fighting for the king in the war which was soon to dislodge the Moors from Granada, their last foothold on Spanish soil. A flurry of diplomatic entreaties failed to change Ferdinand's mind. But when Rodrigo saw fit to intervene to resolve a festering dispute between Ferdinand and Pope Innocent over papal relations with Naples, Ferdinand gratefully released the Vice-Chancellor's eldest son from captivity. Pedro Luis went back to the front line, where he distinguished himself by being the first to breach the Moorish line and enter the Andalusian hilltop fortress town of Ronda. A jubilant King Ferdinand rewarded Pedro Luis by proclaiming the young man Duke of Gandia, a region close to the ancestral Borgia homeland of Jativa. It was a singular honour, for such titles were normally reserved for men of royal blood.

In addition, Ferdinand betrothed Pedro Luis to his own cousin, Maria Enriquez de Luna, who was at the time just nine years old. Pedro Luis returned to Rome in triumph and Rodrigo, who had always shown a predilection for his gentle and kind-natured eldest son, was ecstatic that his favourite was destined for a life as a Spanish grandee. The family's moment of happiness and celebration was, however, peremptorily shattered by Pedro Luis's sudden death in Rome in 1488.

As a soldier ever facing danger, Pedro Luis had been prudent enough to make a will. He bequeathed his dukedom and the estates in Gandia, purchased to match the title, to Juan Borgia, his half-brother and Rodrigo's second son by Vannozza de' Cattanei. Juan, then aged twelve, also inherited the betrothal. He stepped into Pedro Luis's shoes and went to Spain to found a ducal dynasty which was to survive for centuries.

Cesare, now destined to inherit the mantle of Borgia power, was sent in 1489 to study at the University of Perugia in Umbria. Here he showed an enthusiasm for religion which was strangely out of keeping with his ungodly family whose fortunes were vested, nevertheless, in the church. Two years later, Rodrigo transferred Cesare to the University of Pisa specifically to allow him to cultivate a friendship with the powerful Medici family of Florence. Within weeks of this move, Rodrigo induced Pope Innocent to appoint the sixteen-year-old Cesare as bishop of Pamplona, the ancient capital city of the buffer kingdom of Navarre in northern Spain. From that moment, Cesare received the bishop's salary, though he was not to set foot in the city for fifteen years, and then only as a fugitive. The people of Pamplona were enraged at having the unqualified and absent boy foisted on them. Rodrigo's assertion that Cesare had earned the appointment by his 'merits, virtue, and doctrine' did nothing to pacify them and Pope Innocent had to intervene by threatening anyone who opposed Cesare with a papal penalty.

For his treasured daughter Lucrezia, Rodrigo dreamed of a handsome, wealthy, and well-connected Spanish husband. Early betrothals, and even marriages, to cement family links were considered normal, and in February 1491, when Lucrezia was ten years old, her hand was promised to Juan Cherubin de Centelles, Lord of Val d'Ayora, Valencia, a young man born into the highest Spanish nobility. A contract of betrothal was signed which specified that Lucrezia should be sent to Valencia before a year had passed, and marry within six months of her arrival – an accepted way of conducting family business. What was unusual was that devious Rodrigo was in the process of negotiating a second marriage contract with a bridegroom of more impressive credentials even before the first agreement was signed. When the second deal was confirmed, the first betrothal agreement was annulled and another one entered into.

This second nuptial pact, duly signed and sealed in April 1492, promised Lucrezia to Don Gasparo de Procida, son of the Count of Aversa and Almenara and heir to the title. So, within the space of months, the young Lucrezia was engaged to be married to two men. The switch made no difference to her, for she had met neither prospective suitor. However, neither contract was to be fulfilled, for only months after the finalization of the second agreement, Rodrigo's sights would be set even higher.

During Innocent's reign, there was a running battle between the papacy and King Ferrante of Naples. At the centre of the dispute were the three papal cities which lay within the Neapolitan boundaries. Pope Innocent actually agreed to hand over the cities and then vacillated, in the traditional style of Mediterranean negotiators. So Ferrante withheld payment of the papal tribute due from his kingdom, sent an army to Rome, and laid siege to the city. Giuliano della Rovere, Innocent's closest confidant who had even moved into the Vatican to protect his interest, slipped through the besiegers to try to enlist the aid of France's King Charles VIII, himself a rival claimant to the throne of Naples. Rodrigo took advantage of his antagonist's absence to weave a web of influence over the nervous and frightened pope. At Rodrigo's instigation, Ferrante agreed to withdraw his troops and lift the siege in exchange for papal recognition of his hereditary right to his throne. (This was the concordat which won Rodrigo so much favour with King Ferdinand of Aragon – a relative of Ferrante – and the release of Pedro Luis from his imprisonment.) Della Rovere was furious at the success of Rodrigo, his former friend now turned adversary, and regarded him as an arch enemy.

The tiny Tuscan village of Corsignano was blossoming into a papal summer resort, and cardinals were invited to set up homes there. Among the first to build a palace was Rodrigo. His magnificent edifice, designed and constructed by Rosellino, was a subtle blend of medieval and Renaissance styles. It still stands today as the Palazzo Vescoville, and is a centrepiece of the village, which has been renamed Pienza. Rodrigo also arranged for the completion of the work on the chapel in Valencia started by his uncle, Pope Calixtus. He commissioned the spectacular high altar by Andrea Bregno in the church of Santa Maria del Popolo in Rome, while the side chapel frescoes by Pinturicchio were commissioned by Vannozza de' Cattanei. Such patronage achieved its purpose of placing Rodrigo firmly in the public eye. It was all part of his incessant, if subtle, campaign for the papacy.

3

THE GODFATHER POPE

The year 1492 was the crucible of a trio of world-shaking events, each with a strong Spanish connection. Christopher Columbus discovered the Americas in an expedition financed by King Ferdinand of Aragon and his wife Isabella. An Aragonese army wrested Granada from the Moors, who thereby lost their last foothold on Spanish soil. In Rome, Rodrigo Borgia finally became pope.

When the momentous news of the fall of Granada was received by Rodrigo in a personal dispatch from King Ferdinand, the Vice-Chancellor organized a bullfight in the Piazza Navona as a celebration. It was theatrical, and a riveting novelty to Roman eyes.

Two years before Pope Innocent had fallen seriously ill and the purple-robed vultures from the Sacred College started to circle. Rodrigo led the flock as he launched a concerted effort to drum up support for the expected conclave. The general consensus was that Rodrigo would have won overwhelmingly in an election held at that time, but Innocent foiled the hopeful cardinal by surviving the illness.

The wave of support had ebbed by the summer of 1492, when Innocent suffered a savage illness marked by intense abdominal pains and fever. As the malady persisted, it became clear that the pope was dying, and the morbidly expectant cardinals hovered at his bedside. Rodrigo Borgia asked that, as the church's Vice-Chancellor, he be given permission to take over the Castel Sant'Angelo fortress, commanded at the time by Cardinal Giuliano della Rovere, and occupy it on behalf of the College of Cardinals. Innocent was about to agree to the suggestion when della Rovere, the *eminence grise* of his papacy, came in. Della Rovere leaned over the ailing pontiff to whisper that he should remember Borgia was a Catalan and, therefore, unreliable. Rodrigo reacted furiously and snarled across the bed at della Rovere, 'If I were not standing in the presence of His Holiness, I would show you who is Vice-Chancellor.' Della Rovere snorted back. 'If we were not here, I would show you that I am not afraid of you.' Insults flew, and observers of the astonishing scene avowed that a fist fight was prevented only by the ailing pope's presence. Rodrigo Borgia and Giuliano della Rovere, already rivals, were confirmed as irretrievably bitter enemies.

Pope Innocent died on the night of July 25, but the struggle to produce a successor began even before his death as the rival interests started preparing themselves for the battle. This continued during the days of mourning which gave way to the conclave.

As Rodrigo Borgia passed into the sealed-off Sistine Chapel with his companions of the Sacred College on August 6, he was deeply depressed. For he believed that, at sixty-one years of age and after thirty-five years of waiting in the wings as Vice-Chancellor, this was his last chance. And he was firmly convinced that he would lose. Although his service as Vice-Chancellor, an office which was considered a 'second papacy', had shown that he was papal material, most observers and the cardinals themselves agreed that his prospects of election were virtually nil.

Inside the conclave the will of God and the work of the Holy Spirit were, as usual, manifested by the wheelings and dealings among the mercenary members of the Sacred College. The cardinals' machinations reflected the wishes of Italy's princes, who were at each other's throats. The Venetians, citizens of a powerful naval-backed empire, were suspected of seeking territorial aggrandizement at the expense of their neighbour, Milan. The Milanese, therefore, would not countenance a Venice-backed pontiff. The Venetians were equally suspicious of the Milanese, and were averse to anyone tainted by their influence. The Florentines, whose enlightened ruler, Lorenzo, had recently died, spread rumours that the Milanese planned to subjugate the whole of Italy, while the Neapolitans were hostile to all their northern adversaries. Their Aragonese king, Ferrante, was especially tremulous about the Milanese and French claims to his crown.

Each of the rival Italian states hoped for a pope who would favour their own particular interests. Ludovico Sforza, Duke of Milan, primed his brother, Cardinal Ascanio Sforza, to spare no effort or expense in supporting pro-Milanese candidates. King Ferrante of Naples put up a fortune in gold for Giuliano della Rovere to promote cardinals who would serve as Neapolitan agents within the Vatican. Rodrigo, a Spaniard in a conclave dominated by suspicious Italians, was not backed by any of the power groups.

The opening speech of the conclave was made by Cardinal Bernardino Lopez de Carvejal, who compared the church to the 'Whore of Babylon', and begged his colleagues to elect a man who would bring in moral reform. This remark should have brought a flush of colour to Rodrigo Borgia's face, but his immorality does not seem to have worked against him – besides, he was surrounded by men who had led far from saintly lives themselves.

The first inconclusive ballot showed the della Rovere and Sforza candidates splitting the vote to lead, with Rodrigo a surprisingly close third. The second vote produced almost the same result. When the third count was made, deadlock was confirmed and Rodrigo felt his hopes soar. He reasoned that perhaps he could emerge as the compromise candidate all sides would find acceptable.

Della Rovere's hopes were dashed by the very power he had wielded under Pope Innocent. He had manipulated the vacillating old man like a papal puppet, and the other cardinals had viewed his shadowy influence with varying degrees of trepidation. It was this coagulation of fear which decided his fate.

Rodrigo launched a furious campaign to stampede the opposition into support for him. Della Rovere had declared he would prefer anyone to a Borgia pope, and this antago-nism worked in Rodrigo's favour, such was the accumulated mistrust of his rival. He started offering a variety of valuable inducements, scattering them around the Sistine Chapel cells like confetti. On offer were his bishoprics in Spain and Italy, abbeys, fortresses, lands, church benefices of all kinds, papal governorships, and gold. The most potent bribes were his post as Vice-Chancellor, which was certain to fall vacant if he were elected, and his Roman palace. These last two he offered to Cardinal Sforza.

The deliberations continued for five days, but outside the conclave events were conspiring to force a decision from the cardinals. Custom decreed that the rations passed into the sealed Sistine Chapel be cut daily, with the threat that after a week the cardinals' diet would be reduced to bread and water.

Rodrigo worked diligently to appear the perfect com-promise. The Neapolitan men believed him to be anti-Milan, while the Milanese viewed him as anti-Neapolitan. The problem of his Spanish blood receded as he strove to picture himself as an Italianate man, all things to everyone.

Cardinal Sforza succumbed to the temptations offered, and a diarist recorded the spectacle of four mules staggering under loads of silver being transported from Rodrigo's home to Sforza's. Claiming he was switching sides in the interests of compromise, Sforza let it be known that the pro-Milanese faction was switching to Rodrigo. Thus the Borgia victory was assured, and the waverers quickly made their decision so they could accept belated rewards for their support. Even della Rovere, realizing he had nothing to gain and much to lose from further resistance, gave his vote to Rodrigo to present a façade of harmony, and a unanimous decision.

The city of Rome was undergoing the familiar paroxysm of rioting and looting which marred every interregnum, and two hundred people died on the streets in the tumult. Word had spread of the deadlock and many thousands of Romans gathered in the Piazza San Pietro to await the result. An hour before dawn on August 11, the stones blocking a walled-up window on the first floor of the Vatican were pulled aside and a cross emerged. A church prelate began the traditional chant, 'Annuncio vobis gaudium magnum Papam habemus' – 'I announce to you with great joy that we have a pope.' The assembled citizens were astounded to see the figure, diminutive at that distance, standing below the cross. It was Rodrigo Borgia, now Pope Alexander VI.

Alexander, who had donned the papal vestments with the enthusiasm of a child trying on a new suit of clothes, stepped onto the Vatican balcony to intone, 'I am Pope and Vicar of Christ' and offer the traditional benediction, 'I bless the town, I bless the land, I bless Italy, I bless the world.'

Church bells rang throughout the city to herald his election and the victorious Alexander started laying plans for his enthronement, which was to be a spectacle unparalleled since the triumphal processions accorded to the emperors of ancient Rome. The scale of the coronation reflected Alexander's exalted view of himself. A two-mile-long procession walked a carpeted route through the centre of Rome, past houses covered with flags, and winding through arches festooned with the red bull of the Borgia family device grazing in a field of gold. The arches were inscribed with adulatory, almost heretical slogans, 'Alexander the most pious', 'Alexander the invincible', 'Alexander the most magnificent', 'The coronation of the great God Alexander'. Most spectacular of all was an arch erected on the orders of a particularly sycophantic protonotary, which carried in letters of gold the words, 'Rome was great under Caesar, greater far under Alexander. The first was a mortal, the latter is a God.'

The phalanx of the procession was formed by ten thousand cavaliers in colourful dress. Next came every member of the papal household, the foreign ambassadors, and the cardinals, each mounted on horses draped in finery, and each with a twelve-man retinue. The new Captain-General of the Church, the Count of Pitigliano, rode immediately before the pope with his sword drawn, symbolic of his role as defender of the church. Alexander rode under a canopy held aloft by a retinue on foot, and was followed by the papal guard, the Vatican protonotaries and every official of the Curia. Under the scorching heat of the late August Roman sun, the city became a heaving mass of horses and crowds. Despite his years Alexander still possessed a youthful vigour, but the drawn-out ceremonies proved too much even for him. Twice during the day he fainted under the strain. That night a torchlight procession weaved its way through the city, musicians and singers entertained, and bonfires illuminated every piazza.

Alexander, in his own flamboyant style, had opened a new page of history, and a spectator of the coronation observed, 'Antony was not received with as much splendour by Cleopatra as Alexander by the Romans.' Rome was now a Borgia city, and Alexander's wait, concealed in the wings of the Vatican, and his insidious gathering of power, had paid off in the most sensational way.

His shaken adversaries produced an immediate explanation for Alexander's election: he had bought his way into office. Simony, the buying or selling of ecclesiastical posts, is considered amongst the greatest sins in the church, yet it was a sin which every pope for the previous half century at least had committed. The temporal power of the papacy ensured that worldly persuasions were needed to control the church government. These political factors had intervened in the conclave, as they had so often before. Cardinal Sforza had accepted the Vice-Chancellorship and other rewards from Rodrigo Borgia, but only when he realized that the deadlock had to be broken, and because he knew Rodrigo's administrative abilities backed by an astute political brain would be an invaluable asset to the church and Italy during the tumultuous days through which they were passing. Though a Spaniard, Alexander was Italianized enough to seek to outlaw foreign influence from Italy, a cause dear to every native Italian heart.

The ordinary people of Rome were delighted that the generous and popular Rodrigo Borgia had become their pontiff. The Roman barons, fearing the restrictions a strong pope would impose on them, not to mention the threat of Borgia nepotism, were somewhat more apprehensive.

The claims of simony were pressed most by the foreign ambassadors who had failed to spot the possibility of a Borgia once again ascending the throne of St Peter. Many tried to calculate what the papacy had cost Alexander, to list what each cardinal had received for his vote, and singled Cardinal Sforza out in particular as an unscrupulous, greedy man whose boundless thirst for wealth had opened the door for the new pope. The Venetians, alarmed at the prospect of an alliance between the papacy and Milan, made the loudest accusations. The smaller buffer states of Ferrara; Mantua, and Modena were also worried by the possibility of increased Milanese power. King Ferrante of Naples, who had put up so much money to smooth the way for one of his own candidates, wept when he heard of Alexander's election, but he quickly sent a letter of glowing congratulations to make sure his dismay was well disguised. The Sienese were pleased, because they recalled their good relations with Alexander's uncle, Pope Calixtus. Ludovico Sforza, though disappointed that one of his candidates had not won through, was delighted that his brother had so influenced the result and secured for himself the 'second papacy'.

When news of Alexander's election was announced, the youthful Cardinal Giovanni de' Medici showed that he expected the worst. He said, 'Now we are in the power of the wolf, the most rapacious, perhaps, that this world has ever seen; and, if we do not flee, he will infallibly devour us.' This sort of reaction was prompted by jealousy. Alexander's numerous church positions had to be reallocated and they went, as tradition demanded, to his fellow cardinals. And, as always, those cardinals had elected the new pope. If bribery were the most potent force of the conclave, why had Ferrante's gold, offered around by his agent della Rovere, failed to influence the result? The Sacred College had recognized the diligent and hard-working Rodrigo Borgia as their most capable member. Acknowledged as a master diplomat and power manipulator, Alexander was expected to hold a papal balance of power in Italy without the force of arms possessed by the voracious states surrounding the church lands. A papal secretary, Sigismundo die Conti, recognized Alexander's qualifications and wrote, 'It is now thirty-seven years since his uncle, Calixtus III, made him a cardinal, and during that time he never missed a single Consistory [Church Council] unless prevented by illness from attending, which was rare. Throughout the reigns of Pius II, Paul II, Sixtus IV, and Innocent VIII he was always an important personage; he had been Legate in Spain and Italy. Few people understood etiquette as well as he did; he knew how to make the most of himself, and took pains to shine in conversation and be dignified in his manners. In the latter point his majestic stature gave him an advantage. Also he was just at the age, about sixty, at which Aristotle says men are wisest; robust in body, vigorous in mind, he was admirably equipped for his new position.'

During his coronation, Alexander made a firm private promise to Giovanni Boccaccio, ambassador from the Duchy of Ferrara, that he would keep his children at a discreet distance from the papacy. This promise was kept for precisely five days, until Alexander held his first Consistory. At this council, the new pope announced that Cesare Borgia, just seventeen years old, would be appointed to Alexander's archbishopric of Valencia, with its valuable salary and unofficial role as Primate of Spain. He ignored the fact that Cesare had not even been ordained as a priest. Cesare's younger brother Jofre, though only eleven, was given the diocese of Majorca and made an archdeacon of the cathedral of Valencia. A nephew, Juan Borgia-Lanzol, who had earlier been eased into the post of Archbishop of Monreale, was made a cardinal. The other church posts and lands Alexander was obliged to relinquish were passed on, and particular generosity was shown to those who had backed his lunge for power.

All this fuelled the accusations of simony and nepotism, and caused a howl of clerical protest. Alexander studiously ignored the dissent, and a new wave of Borgia opportunists flooded into Rome to join relatives already firmly ensconced there. They were appointed to church jobs, army commands, and palace entourages. In the face of this new Catalan plague, Signor Boccaccio observed, 'Ten papacies would not suffice to satisfy all these relations.'

Anyone seeking the good graces of the pope learned that the way to Alexander's heart lay through Adriana del Mila or Lucrezia. Ambassadors and other supplicants seeking papal favours lavished expensive gifts of jewellery and perfume on the two women to ensure that their entreaties reached Alexander's ears. A contemporary diarist, referring to the home Adriana and Lucrezia shared, commented, 'The majority of those wishing to curry favour with the pope pass through these doors.'

Despite this blatant interference in the affairs of the church state, Alexander developed a reputation as a generous and impartial dispenser of justice. He appointed four commissioners to hear complaints from the ordinary people of Rome, and once a week he sat as commissioner, resolving disputes like a Renaissance Solomon. In a letter to a friend the bishop of Perugia wrote, 'You would be astonished to see how he grants his public audiences to private individuals, even to poor widows, and with what patience and forebearance.'

A facet of Alexander's life which accorded him less credit was his continuing liaison with Giulia Farnese. After his election, it became impossible for him, as pope, to continue his secretive visits to the Monte Giordano palace. For Christ's representative on earth is sure to attract attention wherever he goes. So Alexander cast his eyes around for a palace suitably close to the Vatican which he could use for Giulia's household, and which he could visit without stirring up unwelcome gossip. Just such a palace was the ornamented home of Cardinal Zeno, the palace of Santa Maria in Portico, only yards from the steps of St Peter's. Zeno was persuaded that it was in his best interest to loan the palace to Alexander, and willingly, even gratefully, he did so. A short while after, Adriana del Mila moved in with her daughter-in-law Giulia and Lucrezia. Giulia marked this transition in her life by producing a daughter, Laura, in the same year as Alexander's election. No public or private declaration of paternity was ever made, but the child was generally accredited to Alexander. Visitors remarked in letters afterwards how much the child looked like the pope. Lucrezia was excited about the birth, and spent much of her time helping her friend Giulia nurse the baby. It did not take long for gossip about the child to spread all over Europe. Diarists referred to Giulia as Alexander's concubine, while satirists more dramatically named her the 'Bride of Christ'. When this description reached Giulia's ears, she is said to have responded with a chuckle.

Alexander avowed a flood of good intentions at the beginning of his papacy. He announced that he would restore law and order to Rome and reform the church. A man who clearly believed this promise was Manfredo Manfredi, the envoy from Mantua, a north Italian state, who wrote in a dispatch home, 'The pope has promised to do many things towards the reformation of the court, to dismiss the secretaries and many tyrannical officials, to keep his children away from Rome, and he will make many praiseworthy promotions, and it is said that he will be a glorious pontiff.' But the Florentine envoy, Filippo Valori, reflected a more ambivalent response: 'The Romans and courtiers show little enthusiasm for this promotion. The opinion that is held of the new pontiff is various: many think that he will occupy this chair with great majesty and pomp, since His Holiness is desirous of fame and glory; and to do this he will be the father of all and maintain peace. Many are of the opposite opinion: that to dominate properly he will be an intriguing pope.' Other correspondents fêted Alexander's mental vigour, robust health, and administrative experience, but none could find it within themselves to dwell upon his saintliness or morality.

The leading families of Rome feared the prospect of a strong pope, which Alexander demonstrably was going to be. The inevitable advancement of his large family could only proceed, they knew, at their own expense. Their worst fears were confirmed when Alexander started auctioning off additional Chancellory jobs to carefully selected nonentities, a practice he had held out against before because he felt it would undermine his authority as Vice-Chancellor. A vitriolic satirist echoed the prevalent sentiment when he wrote, 'Alexander sells the keys, the altars, even Christ himself. He has the right to sell them, for he bought them first.'

There was, however, a certain amount of papal reform in the offing. The disgraceful prisons of Rome, administered by the church state, received their first inspections for years. Alexander's apparent friendliness to all was an agreeable surprise to court diplomats. They were also impressed at the way he listened patiently to the petitions of ordinary folk, and at how he might personally intervene on their behalf. Though the celebrated artist Pinturicchio was called in to paint the frescoes in the Vatican papal apartments, Alexander trimmed his household expenditure. His life became almost frugal, and he insisted that only one course should be served at each meal. This was extraordinary in Italy, land of gargantuan appetites, and those who wished to be well fed started finding excuses to evade invitations to the papal dining table.

However, although there had been other nepotistic popes, Alexander was to eclipse them all. For him, family interest was paramount. Like Calixtus before him, he was regarded with suspicion as a devious Catalan operating against the prevalent Italian interest. And, as Calixtus realized, he therefore needed the family support, which he knew he could count on, to keep a firm grip on his temporal domain. Alexander was to take the reigns of power in a vice-like grasp and, with family henchmen at his shoulders, run the papacy like the Mafia. He was the Godfather, with military commanders and administrators totally subservient to his will. Where possible, these underlings were blood relatives, which magnified the degree of his power and control.

Alexander's eldest surviving son Cesare was at Siena preparing a horse for the Palio races while the conclave was deciding the family's future. Cesare realized his ambitious hopes lay in the hands of the gathered cardinals, and his thoughts were concentrated on the unseen events in the Sistine Chapel. He was woken at four in the morning with the electrifying news, brought by an exhausted messenger, that Alexander was the new pontiff. Cesare was so excited that he immediately rode south towards Rome to join in the family triumph. News of his headlong dash reached Alexander, who was already making promises to keep his children away from the Vatican. So the new pope dispatched another courier to divert Cesare to the papal fortress at Spoleto, where he was to await further instructions. Thus Alexander's liveliest and most ambitious son missed the coronation events, waiting until the time seemed prudent to go to Rome.

The young man was already getting a taste for the unbridled power the papacy was to give him. His horse had crossed the line first in the Palio races, but the jockey had engineered this by hurling himself from the steed, thereby lightening the load, some yards from the finish. A virulent objection to this was lodged with the councillors of Siena by Francesco Gonzaga, Marquis of Mantua, the owner of the second horse, and the Marquis was awarded the race. Cesare did not hesitate. He wrote a letter to the councillors pointing out that, as the pope's son, his amity was worth much more to them than the goodwill of a mere marquis of little consequence. He also made it abundantly clear that if his horse was declared the winner, he would regard the matter as a favour which the city could call on him to redeem at a later date. We do not know if the elders of Siena succumbed to this bribery. But this episode confirms the assessment of him by the Florentine Chancellor, Antonio da Colle, as 'very young in all his actions'.

The Florentines had developed a most unfavourable opinion of Cesare, who had been sent to the University of Pisa to study law with enough money to lead an intimidatingly ostentatious existence. Even the Medicis and other leading citizens were quite overwhelmed, and one wrote, 'He has come so well provided with hangings and silver that our not having anything to equal it has left us a little perplexed.'

64

The fact that Cesare proved a brilliant student only served to fuel the hatred felt by his contemporaries. Soon after Alexander became pope, Cesare was again making himself unpopular in Florence by asking favours from Piero de' Medici, who had succeeded his father Lorenzo as the republic's new ruler.

Within months of the election, Alexander considered it prudent to allow Cesare to come to live in Rome. The good-looking and ebullient young man lost no further time in establishing himself as a man about town. He moved into a fine palace in the quarter which had mushroomed around the Vatican and soon had a string of girlfriends, scorning the veritable army of prostitutes which serviced the clerics of the Roman church. But he soon learned to tame his personality, and contemporaries came to admire his eloquence and charm. One wrote, 'Of his mind and tongue he makes what use he will.' Strong and athletic, he was an expert horseman and a matador of formidable reputation. Like his father before him, he dazzled his companions with his luxurious lifestyle.

A view of his glittering presence was left to us by Signor Boccaccio, who wrote, 'The day before yesterday I went to find Cesare at his house in Trastevere. He was on the point of going out for the hunt; he was wearing a worldly garment of silk and had his sword at his side. He had only a little tonsure like a simple priest. I rode at his side and conversed with him at length. I am on intimate terms with him. He possesses marked genius and a charming personality. He has the manners of a great prince; above all he is lively and merry and fond of society; being very modest, his bearing is much better than that of the Duke of Gandia, his brother.' Boccaccio ended with the barbed comment that, though Cesare drew a large salary as Archbishop of Valencia, he had never shown any inclination for the priesthood.

Cesare was to prove invaluable to Alexander. But the pope's other children and relatives were also destined to figure largely in his papacy. Very soon rumours began to spread of the Borgia plans for the future. Cesare, a man of the church by design rather than conviction, was marked for elevation to a cardinalate as a step towards the papacy. His younger brother Juan was to become a military man, and commander of the church army. Lucrezia and Jofre were to be used as dynastic pawns, marrying the Borgias into the royal families of Italy and Spain.

The inevitable takeover of the body of the church started at the outset of Alexander's reign when a great-nephew, Rodrigo Borgia-Lanzol, was handed command of the papal guard. Once the turmoil provoked by this appointment had subsided, Alexander proceeded to pack the Sacred College with his own nominees. As had been suspected, Cesare was a candidate to take the purple of a cardinal, and Alexander set about clearing the final obstacle to this. He published a Papal Bull declaring that Cesare was the legitimate son of the deceased Domenico Rignano and Vannozza de' Cattanei. This meant that when an investigation was made on behalf of the Sacred College, it would be discovered that Cesare was legitimate, and therefore eligible to serve as a cardinal. The very same day Alexander hypocritically signed a private Bull in which he acknowledged that Cesare was, in fact, his own son. It survives to this day, a monument to his duplicity.

Cesare's nomination as a cardinal produced a predictable furore, led by Giuliano della Rovere. The enraged cardinal declared that he would not stand idly by and allow the Sacred College to be thus 'profaned and abused'. So it is easy to imagine the reaction when, at the same time, Alexander declared that he was also proposing that Giulia Farnese's brother Alessandro should become a cardinal. This latter appointment was interpreted as a reward for Giulia's sexual services, and had the whole of the Sacred College up in arms. The voluble howl of disapproval jolted Alexander, who threatened to appoint a majority of new cardinals if the current Sacred College did not defer to his demands. Both appointments were approved, though grudgingly, and Alessandro Farnese (eventually Pope Paul III) became known as 'the petticoat cardinal'. Della Rovere was close to apoplexy, but his continued protest only echoed the impotence he felt.

When Cesare made his formal entry into Rome as a cardinal, every other member of the Sacred College was obliged by papal edict to turn out to greet him. It was an unprecedented, if unwilling, measure of homage to accord to a new cardinal, and announced the power Cesare was destined to wield. Charles VIII, the recently crowned King of France, was quick to ascertain this power, and when he wanted a favoured sycophant, Archbishop Briconnet of St Malo, to be given a cardinalate, he addressed the letter of request to Cesare.

Rome was now clearly a Borgia city, and Giuliano della Rovere could only grind his teeth in an anguish of frustration at the prospect. He led the rival power group in the Sacred College, but any influence he had on affairs was heavily outweighed by the Borgias. However, he still did what he could to weaken Alexander's position. He wrote libellous letters to King Ferdinand of Aragon and many Spanish nobles, assailing the pope's reputation, and these epistles marked the beginning of the destruction of the Borgia name, a cause which was to be worked at by a long line of willing volunteers.

Licking his wounds after his abject defeat, della Rovere slunk away to his impregnable fortress at Ostia, which sat astride Rome's commercial lifeline. While della Rovere controlled the port, Alexander was always nervous, and ordered his finest *condotierri* to watch the gates of Rome for an expected attack. So nervous was Alexander about his adversary's intentions that when a cannon salute to his papal presence boomed out during a journey to a hunting lodge at Ostia, he scurried back to the security of Rome.

Though Cesare was the son who had inherited Alexander's intelligence and self-control, the pope tended to favour the two younger boys, Juan (now the second Duke of Gandia) and Jofre. For Cesare was showing all the signs of possessing the volatile and unpredictable temperament so much a feature of his mother, Vannozza de' Cattanei. When his half-brother, Pedro Luis, died and his will ignored Cesare to leave his Spanish dukedom to Juan, Cesare was angry and disappointed and raged that he would kill Juan. So Juan, whom Alexander found easier to handle, was indulged by his father, and the papal court circle referred to him as 'the spoilt boy'. Consequently vain and arrogant, the handsome Juan became a focus of attention for the court, especially when he rode out in flamboyant Turkish robes.

Juan was to sail to Spain in 1493 to claim his inherited lands and the Spanish royal bride, Princess Maria Enriquez, whom he had been bequeathed by his half-brother. For months before the sixteen-year-old boy set off, Alexander had a goldsmith exclusively employed buying perfect diamonds, rubies, emeralds, and sapphires and setting them in jewellery designed for Juan. In August of that year, an ostentatiously-dressed Juan, dripping with gold and jewels, sailed for the Borgia homeland. The highly suspicious envoy from the north Italian state of Mantua, Gian Lucido Cattaneo, commented in a dispatch, 'The Duke of Gandia leaves very rich and full of jewels, money, and other moveable goods and precious silver. They say he will return within a year, but will leave all that in Spain, and come for another harvest.' The accusation was that the Borgias were looting the Vatican and secreting the booty in Spain. Cattaneo's claim was based on the fleet of four galleys with which Juan sailed, each groaning under the weight of the treasure filling the holds.

The boy also carried with him a letter from his doting father, written in the Valencian dialect. In it, Alexander laid down the law to his son about the conduct expected from him, and warned him of the impression he should strive to make in Spain. 'Be pious, God-fearing, and serve the King faithfully', wrote Alexander. He also adjured the boy to treat his wife well ('be a good companion to her'), not to stay out late at night, and to avoid gambling. Alexander gave a particular warning against embezzling the revenues of the Duchy. Finally he told the boy to pick good administrators and to take heed of their advice. Parental concern extended to the appointment of Jaime Serra, Archbishop of Oristano in Sardinia, as the boy's tutor and adviser, with instructions so detailed they even specified the clothes Juan should wear when he made his official entry into Barcelona.

Alexander must have been fretting about Juan, for before the fleet of galleys had reached Civitavecchia, only a short distance away, a special courier arrived with a second letter. This time the papal father added the advice he had left out the first time. Juan was cautioned about caring for his skin and hair. Alexander said he must put on gloves immediately and leave them on for the duration of the voyage, until he reached Barcelona. 'Salt ruins the skin and in our country people prize beautiful hands.'

Juan soon proved a disappointment to his family. Before he had been away for long, reports filtered back to Alexander denouncing the boy for rakish nights out in taverns, gambling, consorting with prostitutes, and, most serious of all, failing to consummate his marriage. The pope sent sharp letters chastizing Juan for his behaviour, but he also enclosed lavish gifts of money. Cesare also urged his brother to curtail a way of life which was causing their father so much distress. He wrote, 'Try to fulfil the hopes which His Holiness has always founded upon you, if you wish him a long life, in which is all our good, our life and exaltation; and if you have compassion for me, see that these reports that give His Holiness such pain should cease.'

After receiving the letters, Juan took his wife to their home in Gandia. He wrote to Alexander, refuting the tales of his scandalous behaviour, declaring they were propagated by people 'with little brain or in a state of drunkenness'. Juan declared that he had not neglected his wife, and Jaime Serra assured the pope that the boy had consummated his marriage. This was confirmed shortly afterwards by the news that Princess Maria Enriquez was pregnant.

Juan settled down to build a ducal palace in Gandia, which he fitted out in splendid Roman Renaissance style utilizing the opulent furnishings brought on the galleys. The new home was a stark contrast to the drabness of contemporary Spain, and this provoked more complaints which reached the ears of Alexander. Another blistering letter was sent off, in which the pope railed at his son for failing to take into account local feelings.

Alexander's attentions were next focussed on Jofre, the youngest of the family. Mild-mannered and bashful, Jofre disguised a lack of intellect with a winsome smile. The boy was declared legitimate by papal decree at the age of thirteen, just two weeks before he was betrothed to Princess Sancia, a grand-daughter of King Ferrante of Naples. Isabella, the daughter who had married the Roman administrator, was also remembered by Alexander, who looked after her welfare – and his own interest – by promoting her husband Signor Matuzzi to the post of Chancellor of Rome.

Vannozza de' Cattanei had faded into the background of Alexander's life, but he retained a strong affection for her long after their physical relationship had ended. Her husband, Carlo Canale, was made Governor of the Torre di Nona, Rome's prison. Signor Canale was so proud of his link with the Borgias through Vannozza that he even took to signing his name 'de Cattanei' to make sure all were aware of the connection. Vannozza proved a shrewd woman of business and became quite wealthy, owning three inns and a string of houses in Rome. So formidable was her commercial acumen that a man who crossed swords with her over a property deal declared she was 'a woman possessed by the devil'. She continued to write to Alexander, and three of her letters are today contained in the secret archives of the Vatican. Each is a request to see His Holiness, but all are couched in the friendliest of terms, talking about family things like illnesses and news of their grandson, Juan's first child.

Slurs engendered by the pope's overwhelming interest in family business circulated throughout Rome. Alexander heard of this invective, but made no attempt to curb it. He shrugged his shoulders and said, 'Rome is free territory, and Romans have a habit of saying and writing whatever takes their fancy.'

4

A HUSBAND FOR LUCREZIA

Alexander loved his daughter Lucrezia to distraction – she had long-blonde hair, earnest blue eyes, and her gaiety infected all who met her. Signor Boccaccio, the Ferrarese ambassador, wrote, 'She had a smile that lit up her features in a thousand different ways. Never did a gentle creature seem happier to be alive.' Her walk was so light that she seemed to float along, her feet hardly touching the ground.

Her earliest memories of life were of her mother, Vannozza de' Cattanei, and her three-storey house with its oak-beamed ceilings and whitewashed walls. Vannozza had been widowed by then, so it was natural for Lucrezia to call the berobed man with the resonant voice who regularly visited their home 'Papa'. She came to look forward eagerly to his visits, and Cardinal Rodrigo de Borgia doted on the girl as he watched her learning to play the lute, dance, draw and embroider intricate designs in gold and silver.

The Roman lawmakers, justifiably suspicious that step-fathers might try to appropriate the inheritances of their new children, had wisely stipulated that the guardianship of a widow's children should be passed on. So it was compara-tively easy for Rodrigo to arrange for his children by Van-nozza to be taken into the care of the reliable Adriana del Mila. Lucrezia's family orbit had thereby switched to the Monte Giordano palace overlooking the Tiber, where her playmate was the sweet-tempered Giulia Farnese. Rodrigo, now elevated to the papacy, took a fatherly delight in watch-ing Lucrezia flower into womanhood.

When Lucrezia moved to the palace of Santa Maria in Portico with Adriana and Giulia, her obvious and radiant happiness still charmed all who met her. One visitor wrote a letter home declaring, 'She is of middle height and graceful of form, her face is rather long, the nose well-cut, hair golden, her mouth is rather large, the teeth brilliantly white, her neck is slender and fair, her bosom admirably proportioned. She is always gay and smiling.' Father and daughter adored each other, but in this period of history even the most loving of fathers regarded their daughters as marketable commodities to help secure diplomatic treaties or to increase the family wealth.

Alexander studiously ignored the prior claims of Don Gasparo de Procida, her second Spanish fiancé, which had been solemnly acknowledged in a betrothal only months before, and started negotiations for a match more in keeping with his present situation. Undertones of hostility from Naples persuaded Alexander that an alliance between the papacy, Milan, and Venice would give a degree of welcome security. Accordingly, he had Cardinal Ascanio Sforza arrange a marriage contract between Lucrezia and the widowed twenty-eight-year-old Lord of Pesaro, Giovanni Sforza, a cousin of the Milanese ruling family. Giovanni came to Rome in October 1492 on a mission so secretly guarded that the ambassadors to the papal court believed he was there to arrange a match for someone else. He was able to keep news of his betrothal to Lucrezia under wraps, and fooled everybody except Don Gasparo de Procida, who was by now living in Italy.

Don Gasparo descended on Rome in a fury and provoked a showdown with Pope Alexander by claiming his bride on the same day that the new match was being agreed. Signor Boccaccio reported, 'There is much gossip about Pesaro's marriage. The first bridegroom is still here, raising a great hue and cry, as a Catalan, saying he will protest to all the princes and potentates of Christendom; but will he, nil he, he will have to submit.' Boccaccio was right. The voluble presence of Don Gasparo could, Alexander realized, prove a damaging embarrassment. But the pope, a prince among negotiators, knew the way to an aggrieved suitor's heart. He agreed to pay-off of three thousand gold ducats, Don Gasparo agreed to an annulment of his claims, and the placated suitor moved back to Spain.

Three months later, the nuptial agreement with the Lord of Pesaro was signed in a formal ceremony in the Vatican. Alexander agreed to pay a dowry of thirty thousand gold ducats and appoint Giovanni Sforza to a *condotta* in the church army. He was content with the match, which he con sidered useful politically, and which he saw as securing Lucrezia's future in an Italian royal house. Pesaro was a small fief of the papacy in the Romagna, and its rule was typical of the despotic, tyrannical governments which succeeded the democratic city-states of the Middle Ages. Giovanni Sforza was absolute ruler and his word was law. The elder of two illegitimate sons of the previous Lord of Pesaro, he had governed since his father's death. So pleased was Giovanni with his prospective bride that he invited the whole of Pesaro high society to a ball at his palace. A guest later wrote, 'They danced in the great hall, and the couples hand in hand issued from the castle led by Monsignor Scaltes, the pope's plenipotentiary, and the people in their joy joined in and danced away the hours in the streets of the city.'

Lucrezia's latest prospective husband was a tense, humourless man with a cold and pinched nature and a grim expression around his eyes and mouth. Not that such things were yet known to her, for she would not set eyes on the man she was to swear to spend the rest of her life with until the day of their wedding. In the meantime, Lucrezia started assembling her trousseau and the gold and silver plate she was to take to her new home. Ambassadors of the Italian princes paying courtesy calls on Lucrezia to gain favour with Alexander vied with each other to shower her with gifts of pearls, rubies, diamond rings, carved mirrors, gold embroidered pillowcases, even a silver lavabo. When the gifts were laid out in the Vatican for inspection by the guests on her wedding day, the room looked like Aladdin's cave.

Giovanni Sforza's purse could not match Alexander's, and he was forced to scrape together what money he could to keep up appearances for the wedding Using Lucrezia's still-unpaid dowry as security, he raised the money to meet expenses, and borrowed a gold collar studded with pearls and rubies to wear on the wedding day. He rode south to Rome accompanied by one hundred and twenty men at arms, fifty horsemen, and several bishops.

When he arrived at the Porta del Popolo on June 12, 1493 he was greeted by every member of the Roman Senate, the ambassadors to the papal court, and his three future brothers-in-law, Cesare, Juan and Jofre. He rode at the head of the wedding procession as it wound its way through Rome, across the Ponte Sant'Angelo, and past the front of the palace of Santa Maria in Portico. Trumpets heralded his approach and Lucrezia, excitedly awaiting this moment, ran to one of the loggias overlooking the Piazza San Pietro. It was the first time she had appeared in public, and the gathered crowd strained to catch a glimpse of her. She hardly noticed the crowd as she in her turn strained her eyes to look at the distant figure of her bridegroom. Giovanni spotted his thirteen-year-old bride, reined in his horse, and saluted her in knightly fashion with his sword. Lucrezia curtsied and giggled, then hurried back into the palace with Giulia Farnese and Adriana del Mila. Giovanni rode on to the Vatican, where he prostrated himself at his prospective father-in-law's feet to dedicate his own and Pesaro's allegiance to the pope.

Alexander had decided that Lucrezia should be married in his Vatican apartments, which were newly decorated but still unfurnished. Frescoes by Pinturicchio covered the walls and vaulted ceilings. The centrepiece, a fresco entitled *The Disputation of St Catherine,* was pure Borgia egotism. Lucrezia was depicted as St Catherine, while Rodrigo Borgia appeared both as a young Bishop and a pious Pope Alexander VI, kneeling in prayer. For the occasion, the blank walls were hung with velvet and tapestries. The great papal throne was covered with brocade and set in the centre of the Great Hall for the ceremony. Chairs covered in velvet and brocade were set out for the bride, groom and witnesses. There were one hundred and fifty other guests drawn from the leading families of Rome, seated on cushions scattered around the floor.

When Juan Borgia went to collect Lucrezia and escort her to the ceremony, his gold Turkish robe looked even more splendid than her wedding dress, which had a train carried by a Negro slave girl. Lucrezia walked into the Great Hall on Juan's arm, followed by Giulia and Adriana del Mila. Alexander sat on his elevated throne as Lucrezia, Giovanni Sforza, his sons – including Cesare, dressed in ecclesiastical black – and everyone else who had gathered for the ceremony walked in line before him. All the women curtsied graciously, and Lucrezia and Juan then stepped forward to kiss Alexander's feet, followed by all the other guests.

When Lucrezia and her bridegroom knelt on cushions before Alexander to make their vows, the supposedly celibate pontiff showed not a flicker of embarrassment at the fact that he was performing his daughter's marriage ceremony in the precincts of the church's most holy place. Alexander asked the couple if they would take each other as man and wife, and although they had never exchanged a word with each other, both affirmed that they would do so 'most willingly'. The Bishop of Concordia knelt before the couple to slip the wedding ring on Lucrezia's ring finger on her left hand and another on her index finger. Until this point in the proceedings the commander of the papal army held an unsheathed sword over the couple's heads. This was a Renaissance tradition, designed to graphically remind the bride what lay ahead of her if she did not observe her marriage vows. Once the rings were securely in place the sword was lowered and resheathed, as if the warning had by now been sufficiently made.

A sermon from the bishop on the sacrament of marriage ended the service, and Juan Borgia stepped forward to take his sister's arm and lead her into the adjoining room for the strange ceremony of the sweets. Johannes Burchard, the papal master of ceremonies, wrote in his diary, 'An assortment of all kinds of sweets, marzipan and drinks of wine in about a hundred basins and cups was brought and carried around with napkins by chamberlains and grooms. They first served the pope and the cardinals, then the bridegroom and the ladies, whilst others went to the clergy and the rest, and finally they flung what sweets remained amongst the people outside, in such abundance that more than a hundred pounds of sweets were crushed and trampled underfoot.' Such sweets were extremely rare, and considered a great luxury. The papal purse-holders were furious at this squandering of church resources, for the whole cost of the extravaganza was met out of Vatican funds. A mound of left-over sweets were tossed into the air above the gathered guests, and the diarist Stefan Infessura complained disgustedly, 'And this in honour of almighty God and the Roman church'.

The wedding was also contrary to the all-male tradition in the Vatican, for the medieval church viewed women as Eve personified, on this earth to divert men from God's chosen path. Their very presence within the portals was regarded as a sign of the debasement of the church. Earlier pontiffs – like Pius II, who had possessed many mistresses and fathered a number of children – had turned their backs on their women and offspring when they ascended the papal throne. Alexander was to be quite different from any of his predecessors in this matter. He was far too fond of women and his children to remove them from his life. His myriad critics led by the fuming Giuliano della Rovere were to use this as ammunition to try to undermine his position.

A select few stayed at the Vatican for an evening wedding banquet, where the marriage gifts were presented to Lucrezia and her husband. Each of the cardinals had a lady seated at his side. After the meal, the guests drifted out into the gardens of the Vatican, where musicians played and couples danced until late at night. Letters from church officials and ambassadors scandalized by this licentious behaviour went to all parts of Europe.

When the celebrations finally ended Alexander escorted the couple on foot the short distance back to the palace of Santa Maria in Portico. It was customary at the time for such dynastic marriages to be consummated in front of witnesses, but this was dispensed with because of Lucrezia's youth. In fact, the couple did not sleep together for some time for that very reason, though they both lived in the Santa Maria palace. The delay in consummation of a marriage was not unusual, but did not present any great problem for the bridegroom – meanwhile he was expected to vent his passion on courtesans. A strict double standard was maintained, however, and the wife was expected to remain faithful, particularly as the husband wanted to be sure that any offspring produced by his spouse were fathered by him.

Under the terms of the nuptial contract Lucrezia and Giovanni Sforza were to live in Rome for a year after the wedding, and they remained at Santa Maria in Portico, where the household was ruled firmly by Adriana del Mila. For a time, Giovanni seemed content enough with his existence in Rome, where he became something of an exalted citizen. Shortly after his marriage, he was chosen to ride out with Juan Borgia, Duke of Gandia – 'as if they were two kings' wrote one observer – as a deputation to welcome King Ferdinand's ambassador, Don Diego Lopez de Hare, who had been sent to remonstrate with Alexander about the simony and dishonesty rampant in the Vatican, and also to complain that the Jews who had been expelled from Aragon were being welcomed in Rome.

Giovanni's finances were improved because he was drawing salaries both from the Milanese army funds and from his *condotta* with the church army. In the meantime, a proposed alliance between the papacy, Milan and Venice had been designated the League of St Mark, and the smaller buffer states of Mantua, Ferrara, and Siena scurried to join as a sign of loyalty to ensure their own protection.

However, it was not long before the apparent comfort of Giovanni's existence began to feel like a bed of nails to him. The overbearing personality of Adriana del Mila meant he could never feel master at Santa Maria in Portico, and he felt threatened by the obvious warmth between Alexander and Lucrezia. He wanted to take her to his home-ground at Pesaro, where he could feel more in control of his situation, but he was so dependent on the austere and powerful Alexander's goodwill that he felt unable to make any move to assert his own will. This conflict raged inside him and did nothing to improve his already somewhat sour personality.

Giovanni partly eased his frustration when, complaining about the oppressive, muggy high summer Roman days and the risk of plague, he obtained Alexander's permission to return on his own to Pesaro. But he found problems awaiting him there. For the creditors who had loaned him money to finance his wedding preparations were by now pressing for payment. There was no way he could raise the funds from his tiny state, so he wrote a plaintive appeal to Alexander, asking to be paid part of Lucrezia's contracted dowry to meet his commitments. The pope discussed the request with Giovanni's cousin, Cardinal Ascanio Sforza, and replied to the young lord informing him that when the Roman weather was cooler and healthier he should return to the city to consummate his marriage. The reward for this service would be not part, but the whole of the dowry.

This bait would, on the face of it, seem irresistible to a man faced with mounting financial problems, but Giovanni displayed a distinct reluctance to return to Rome. Perhaps he was suspicious about Alexander keeping his word. Or perhaps the young man's disinclination can be explained by the way such marriages were arranged without either partner having any choice in the matter. In those circumstances, a lack of physical desire is understandable, and the embarrassment of a youthful bride would not help. The groom had had experience with his first wife and with many courtesans and mistresses, but men were warned by their elders not to seek from their wives the sort of satisfaction they reaped from mistresses. Sex within marriage was intended for procreation only. Wives were advised firmly not to show undue enthusiasm for their husbands, for this might make them seem like whores. Passionate sex was also believed to be unfruitful. The end product of these oft-repeated admonitions was that married couples regarded their sexual relations as something of a chore, and thoughts of this nature might well have been filling Giovanni's head as he lingered in Pesaro.

The allure of Alexander's gold did eventually overpower Giovanni's resistance and in November 1493 he went back to live in the Santa Maria palace. Within a few days of being reunited with his young wife he left on a tour of the papal lands with Alexander and Cesare. The trio made a triumphal entry into Orvieto and stayed for a series of ceremonies, parties, and banquets which usually degenerated into drunken discussions of affairs of state. After spending Christmas with Lucrezia and her family, Giovanni was presented with his gold reward and Alexander was content to allow the young man to return to Pesaro, ostensibly to look after the government of his lands. The pope was pleased that his daughter remained in Rome close to him, and Lucrezia, who had seen Giulia Farnese's marriage in all its empty detail, did not expect overmuch from her own. She was never in love with her husband, nor he with her, and she may have realized that this was something she had no right to expect.

It was not until the early summer of 1494 that Giovanni Sforza returned once again to Rome to collect Lucrezia and take her to Pesaro, as allowed for in the marriage agreement. Alexander would have preferred to keep his daughter near to him, but he realized he could delay the inevitable no further. Naturally Lucrezia was upset at her first separation from her father, but she was accompanied by Adriana del Mila and Giulia Farnese. The road from Rome to Pesaro passed through difficult terrain infested by bandits, and the party, travelling in bone-jolting carriages based on artillery carts, was obliged to seek shelter in primitive inns along the way to avoid the risk of being set upon by brigands in open country after dark. Alexander worried about their safety, and the three women tried to assuage his fears by keeping him regularly informed of their progress, telling him of the warm welcomes they received at towns along the way, where local dignitaries prudently strove to show their loyalty and devotion to their protector, the pope.

5

A BATTLE OF WITS

From the moment that Charles VIII succeeded to the throne of France, the dwarfish, hideously ugly monarch dreamed of becoming a conquering emperor. He wanted to reclaim the Neapolitan lands his ancestors had ruled until 1442, only a few decades before, when the Aragon royal house had snatched the sovereignty. Charles had inherited a powerful army and a firmly united country, and he regarded Italy, which was economically rich but fragmented and weak, as ready to be seized.

Only days after Alexander was elected pope, the French ambassador to the Holy See, Perron de Baschi, asserted Charles's claim to the throne of Naples and demanded a papal investiture to concede church legality to his monarch. Alexander had expected just such an approach, and said that he would be willing to investigate the claims of the Angevin royal line to the Neapolitan throne, but warned that this would take time. Monsieur de Baschi informed the pope that Charles was seeking permission for French troops to move unmolested through the papal lands, the gateway for a planned invasion of Naples. Alexander said that this might be possible, but that the question of permission would have to be held in abeyance until the papal decision of the investiture was reached.

Alexander had, in fact, already decided that he would not back the French claims. The Aragon royal hold on the throne of Naples had, after all, been confirmed again and again by previous popes, and Alexander did not see how he could overturn such an oft-repeated ruling. Added to that, he was a Spaniard himself, with a special link of allegiance to the

Aragon kings, and did not want to upset the support he derived from that direction. Perhaps most important of all, Alexander saw clearly that French control of Naples would imprison the papacy. Not that Alexander conveyed his thoughts and fears to Monsieur Baschi. While stalling for time, he diplomatically left his decision on the issue open.

King Ferrante of Naples could not read the workings of Alexander's devious mind, and believed the pope was planning to abandon him in face of the French pressure. He felt threatened when the League of St Mark was formed, and misread it as an alliance directed against him, so confusing was the turbulent state of Italian politics. Ferrante sent a letter of protest to his relative, King Ferdinand of Aragon, spelling out the joint threat he felt from the existence of the League and the French claims to his throne, which he suspected Alexander was about to support. A short while after this, Ferdinand sent a special envoy to Rome, supposedly to clear this matter up with Alexander. But the representative was there, in reality, on a top-secret mission to seek papal approval for the Aragonese sovereignty over the New World discoveries, which were threatened by a surge of Portuguese expansionism.

In response to this visit Alexander issued the historic Papal Bulls dividing the Americas between the two Iberian countries, with a very strong bias in Spain's favour. The line he drew is reflected today in the map of South America, where on one side, in countries such as Argentina and Chile, Spanish is spoken, and on the other side, countries such as Brazil are ruled by Portuguese speaking people. This papal obedience to Ferdinand's wishes strengthened Alexander's ties with the Aragon royal household and led Ferdinand to reaffirm the betrothal of Princess Maria Enriquez to Juan Borgia.

King Ferrante was so jumpy that he now started to suspect even Ferdinand of collusion with the papacy against him. For Naples had been ruled directly from Spain until 1458 when the empire was split and the illegitimate son of Alfonso V of Aragon placed on the Neapolitan throne. Ferrante was graphically aware that Ferdinand nursed a grievance about the lost dominions. The question he now pondered was how much Ferdinand was prepared to gamble to regain Naples.

Provoked by a state of panic, Ferrante moved his army up to the border with the Papal States, an exercise in sabre-rattling designed to warn Alexander against permitting the French attempt to usurp his throne. The threat made no difference to the pope, who had already decided to continue the papal blessing to Ferrante's sovereignty. But Ferrante was so confused that he then tried to bribe Alexander into compliance, by offering his grand-daughter, Princess Sancia, as a bride for Jofre Borgia, and including the titles of Prince of Squillace and Count of Cariati, too. Alexander was well aware why the offer was made, but nevertheless he accepted it wholeheartedly. This made Ferrante breathe a little easier.

King Charles, however, entertained no illusions about the direction in which Alexander was moving. He piled on the pressure, threatening to hold up the church revenues derived from France, and to call a council to depose the pope, knowing he could call on the support of the disenchanted faction of the Sacred College led by Cardinal Giuliano della Rovere.

In January 1494 King Ferrante died and Alexander was forced into making a decision. He had either to recognize the legal accession of Ferrante's son Alfonso, or to abandon his link with the Aragon royals. He chose the former, and a French invasion became inevitable.

Alexander combined papal acknowledgement of Alfonso's claims with a ferocious denunciation of the threatened French intervention, which had been kept in an advanced state of readiness by King Charles. Two days later Alexander announced the appointment of his nephew Juan Borgia-Lanzol, Cardinal of Monreale, as the papal Legate who was to be sent to Naples to crown Alfonso. King Charles responded by publicly declaring war against the newly-proclaimed monarch. Cesare Borgia was assigned by Alexander to try to negotiate with the French and chase away the spectre of war hanging over Italy.

It was a fruitless task. Charles wanted the Neapolitan

throne, either peacefully or, failing that, after a war. He left no room for compromise. At the same time Cesare was handling the dealings with Alfonso over Jofre Borgia's coming marriage to Princess Sancia, and persuaded the Neapolitan king to tie a yearly salary of forty thousand gold ducats to his younger brother's titles. In addition, church benefices and state lands were secured for both Cesare and Juan Borgia. It was altogether a very expensive business, but King Alfonso knew he was paying out an insurance premium on a survival policy. The Borgias were delighted with the bonuses the negotiations had won for them, and Cesare wrote to Juan Borgia in Spain, 'We have good reason, my lord brother, to kiss continually the ground on which His Holiness walks and to pray always for the life of him who has made us so great; and therefore I pray you to continually serve and please His Holiness, in a manner that you may show him on our behalf our gratitude in everything that we can.'

Alfonso was crowned by Cardinal Juan Borgia-Lanzol in Naples on May 8, 1494. It was a magnificent occasion, orchestrated by Johannes Burchard, the Vatican's own accomplished master of ceremonies. Three days later it was Jofre Borgia's turn as he was married to the beautiful, green-eyed Princess Sancia. Their nuptial banquet continued until three o'clock in the morning when the bridal couple were escorted to their bedroom, undressed by the bridesmaids, and put into bed together naked. Then for half an hour under the interested gaze of King Alfonso, Cardinal Borgia-Lanzol, Jofre's retinue and the bridesmaids, the thirteen-year-old bridegroom and his fifteen-year-old princess kissed and cuddled, apparently without any embarrassment. At an appropriate moment – even stern tradition demanded some modesty – the couple were left to complete the consummation of their marriage in private. Cardinal Borgia-Lanzol asserted in a later report to Alexander that Jofre's performance had been gracious and full of spirit, and he declared that he would have paid heavily for others to have seen the young bridegroom as he had.

The couple honeymooned on one of Jofre's new feudal estates in Naples, but their happiness was to prove short-lived. Jofre was a weak character who proved no match for the wilful and headstrong Sancia. Soon reports were filtering back to Rome detailing her prolific amorous adventures, while Jofre was compensating with extravagant spending sprees. Alexander was sad that the youngest member of the family was being used so badly, and sent a series of indignant letters to Sancia, accusing her of outrageous immorality. A firm response and defence of the princess came from her steward, who assured the pope that the only man, apart from her husband, who entered her bedroom was 'a man of good will, well past his sixtieth birthday'. Alexander was only too aware of the possibilities open to men of that age with young women. However, he could not allow the matter to hold his attention, for a more pressing dilemma was brewing for him in the north.

Alexander had hoped a firm alliance with Milan through the League of St Mark would block the invasion route for a French attack on Italy. But the League proved to be un-stable, rocked by internal dissent, mutual suspicion, and incessant squabbling between the member states. It was a typically volatile, unpredictable, and unreliable Italian fed-eration. Added to this, there was bad blood between the ruling houses of Milan and Naples. Ludovico Sforza, who coveted the title of Duke of Milan held by his indolent and timid nephew, Gian Galeazzo, had imprisoned the young man and his wife in a castle at Pavia, while taking executive control of the state for himself. Duke Galeazzo was married to Isabella d'Aragona, a grand-daughter of the Neapolitan monarch who was naturally incensed about the treatment of her and her husband. Ferrante had asked Alexander to help topple the usurper Ludovico and return the power to the rightful heir to the dukedom.

So Ludovico was eager to help strengthen any blow aimed at Naples and proved a willing accomplice when King Charles approached him. He announced that he backed the French monarch's claim to the Neapolitan throne and that if

Charles was obliged to snatch his hereditary right by force of arms then the French army would be given free passage through Milan. This declaration opened the door to Italy for Charles, and an epidemic of panic swept through the many courts up and down the peninsula. Venice, believing the battle to be lost in one blow because of Ludovico's compliance, and that resistance would be futile, declared a prompt neutrality.

Alexander, deeply committed to the Aragon cause, dug his heels in and announced that the French would have to fight every inch of the way through papal territory. His boldness terrified the barons of the Romagna, who knew how poorly equipped they were to resist an invasion in force. Many of his warlords had little sympathy for Alexander, and he realized that he could not count on their loyalty. Florence saw the gravity of the French threat to Italy, and sided with the papacy, but, as Alexander knew, the city-state was a military nonentity which Charles could soon conquer. Desperately, Alexander even appealed to the sultan of Turkey for aid, despite the fact that the Ottoman empire was Moslem and therefore anti-Christian. No help was forthcoming from this quarter, for the sultan had problems of his own keeping his turbulent lands in order. However, one of Alexander's letters to the sultan was intercepted by French agents, and its contents used to blacken his name, especially among Italy's rulers.

The only other ally Alexander could rely on was Naples, the final target of the aggressive French intentions. Alexander met with Alfonso, the new king, in July 1494 to coordinate plans for their joint resistance. As the storm clouds gathered, Alexander and Cesare made a tour of the northern papal cities, presented as a series of courtesy calls. In fact, these cities lay on the route the French were expected to take, and the two men were checking on their security arrangements in the event of a French army arriving outside the walls. With them on the tour they took Giulia Farnese, whom they collected from the Farnese family seat at Capodimonte – even while undergoing the severest political traumas of his life, Alexander was a man who found it difficult to dispense with his creature comforts. When the papal entourage returned to Rome, Cesare was entrusted with the task of preparing the city's defences.

Meanwhile King Charles was plunging deep into the French coffers to raise the money for his army, and preparation for the war. He signed peace treaties with his traditional enemies England, the Holy Roman Empire, and Aragon, although King Ferdinand declared this would make no difference to his support for his kinsmen in Naples. However, it was clear that such support would not be of a military nature.

The opening days of September 1494 saw King Charles riding through the Alps at the head of the biggest army assembled in Europe for more than a century. It consisted of thirty thousand men, spearheaded by German and Swiss infantry mercenaries, who were the most feared soldiers in the world. The soldiers' spirits were boosted by the news that Louis d'Orleans, cousin of the French king, had led his country's fleet to a comprehensive defeat of the Neapolitan navy off Genoa. Ludovico Sforza personally welcomed the French columns into Milan, and was himself cheered a few days later when he heard that his nephew had died in his castle prison, allowing him to claim the ducal crown and finally become the recognized master of Milan.

Italy trembled at the feet of the diminutive King Charles. Florentine resistance crumbled without a shot being fired, and the insipid Piero de' Medici grovelled at his meeting with the French monarch. This spectacle so enraged the proud Florentines that they rose to sack the Medici palace and threw Piero out of the city. The Florentine coastal city of Pisa took advantage of the resultant dislocation to claim its independence, which severed the republic's economic lifeline. Into the confusion stepped the Dominican monk and religious fanatic Savonarola. A fiery preacher, Savonarola had predicted that Charles would come to cleanse the sins of Italy. Because the Florentines believed his consequent influence with Charles would prevent the destruction of their city, the monk was invited to take over control.

The invasion took on the air of a procession as the French forces moved unresisted through Italy. Duke Ercole of Ferrara allowed them to pass untouched through his domain, a compliant move which brought tears to a shaken Alexander's eyes as he told the Ferrarese ambassador, 'Italy ought to be left to the Italians, and every man ought to feel safe in his own state.'

In mid-campaign King Charles declared that his true motive for taking Naples under his wing was to enable him to launch a crusade against the Turks from a base in southern Italy. Citing this spurious reason to Alexander, he requested permission to move his army through the Papal States. Alexander's refusal was immediate and resolute, but it made no difference. The allied Neapolitan and papal troops, ranged in the Romagna to the east of the Apennine mountain chain, were outflanked by the simple expedient of Charles taking the more direct route to Rome on the west. As Charles charged south, Alexander's position deteriorated rapidly. It became hopeless when the Colonna family, backed by other rebellious Roman barons, took the fortress commanding the mouth of the River Tiber at Ostia from papal troops and surrendered it to the French. Alexander held his ground, bravely declaring he would rather die than become the slave of the king of France. His situation was hopeless, and by now he had come to believe that Charles was intent not only on capturing Naples, but also planned to bring the whole of Italy under his domination.

Alexander's attention was temporarily diverted from the French crisis by the women in his life. Rumours that Lucrezia was gravely ill, and even that she had died, reached him in Rome. Desperately worried, he sent couriers racing through the hills to Pesaro, where Lucrezia was staying at her husband's home, to find out the truth. It transpired that Lucrezia had been ill, but much less severely than Alexander had been led to believe. Relieved to hear that his daughter had fully recovered, Alexander wrote to her, 'Donna Lucrezia, our dearest daughter, truly you have given us four or five days of great sorrow and anxiety, by reason of the dreadful and bitter rumour which spread throughout Rome, that you were either dead or truly so sick that your life was despaired of. You may guess what agony our mind sustained, by reason of that warm and boundless love we bear you, as much as any person in this world. We give thanks to God and Our Lady in Her glory that you escaped all danger; and be assured we shall not rest content until we have seen you in person.'

The same courier carried an epistle for Giulia, who had been staying with Lucrezia and Adriana del Mila, which was part love letter and part a remonstration against what he considered her too-fulsome praise of Caterina Gonzaga, a relative of Giovanni Sforza. He wrote, 'We know well that your expatiating and dilating on the beauty of this person, who is not worthy so much as to untie your shoes, is due to the modesty you affect, in this as in all other matters. We are well aware, too, why you acted thus; so that you, being informed that all who wrote to us said that beside you she seemed but a lantern held against the sun, we might the more appreciate your beauty, of which, to tell the truth, we never doubted. And we would wish that just as we know this clearly, so you for your part were wholly destined and made over, with no reserves, to that person who loves you more than anything else in the world.'

The letter he had received from his 'Bride of Christ' clearly rekindled Alexander's longing for her presence, for he wrote a letter to Adriana warning her of the impending French menace, and ordering her to return forthwith to Rome with Lucrezia and Giulia. The reply he received was from Lucrezia, who explained that Adriana and Giulia had left in a hurry for the Farnese home at Capodimonte after getting word that Giulia's brother Angelo was dying. Cesare received a similar letter from his sister, which Alexander read and believed to contain a different explanation for the sudden departure. His suspicions were aroused, and he wrote angrily to Lucrezia, 'But of a truth, Don Giovanni and yourself have displayed very little thought for me in this departure of Madonna Adriana and Giulia, since you allowed them to leave without our permission. For you should have remembered, indeed, it was your duty, that such a sudden departure without our knowledge would cause us the greatest displeasure. And if you say that they did so because Cardinal Farnese commanded it, you ought to ask yourself whether it would have pleased the pope. However, it is done. But another time we will be more careful, and will look about to see where our interests lie.'

He wrote a letter to Giulia at Capodimonte which betrayed the jealousy he was feeling, and she responded, 'Since Your Holiness writes exhorting me strongly to act as befits me, to watch my virtue, in these matters I can at once set Your Holiness's mind at rest. Be assured that day and night I have no other thought in my mind – both for my own honour and for love of Your Holiness – than to show myself another St Catherine.' To further try to calm her lover's seething emotions, Giulia assured him that Adriana del Mila would confirm her faithfulness.

Couriers were kept fully employed running numerous letters between Giulia and Alexander over the following weeks. In response to one from his absent mistress, the pope wrote, 'Giulia, dearest daughter, I received your letter which, if it had been longer and more prolix, would have made me even happier.' Giulia started filling her letters with a mixture of affection and excited descriptions of the beautiful surroundings at the lakeside Capodimonte castle. In one, addressed 'To my one and only lord', she sought to impress on Alexander how much she missed him by saying, 'And since perchance Your Holiness may believe, reading the above-mentioned things, that we are in great joy and happiness, we do certify this as a great error, since being absent from Your Holiness, and all my happiness and well-being depending thereupon, I cannot taste such delights with any satisfaction. Wheresoever my treasure is, there shall my heart be also. And he who says the contrary is right foolish. So we beseech Your Holiness, do not forget us . . . and if Your Holiness pleases to remember us, bring us back soon to kiss the feet we miss and long for.'

In the meantime Giulia's husband, Orsino Orsini, had been ordered to link up with the Duke of Calabria's Neapolitan forces in the Romagna, and left his family estate at Bassanello to do so. However, he quickly fell ill and returned home, then wrote to Giulia at Capodimonte, instructing her to join him. She in turn wrote to Alexander, saying her husband had called on her to go to his home. Alexander, feeling the painfully jealous pangs of an absent lover, suspected that Orsino had faked his illness in an attempt to reclaim his wife. Worse, he felt that Giulia actually wanted to go to her husband, preferring the limp-brained young man to himself. A letter sped from the Vatican to Capodimonte. Under no circumstances, Alexander told his mistress, could he countenance her going to Bassanello. The matter was for him beyond discussion. Giulia wrote back, suggesting a political reason for going to Orsino's home. Alexander then wrote to Cardinal Alessandro Farnese, ordering him to intervene and tell his sister that she must return to Rome, and must under no circumstances go to Bassanello. The cardinal felt embarrassed at being in the centre of a tug of war. Absolute obedience to her husband's wishes was expected from a Renaissance wife, but how did that duty match up to a demand from the pope, especially a pope to whom he owed his very position in life? He felt unable to tell Giulia to ignore her husband's wishes, and suggested a compromise to Alexander. He proposed that Orsino should be ordered to Rome, then Giulia could follow him there.

This only confirmed Alexander's opinion that the girl was trying to evade him in favour of her husband. He wrote Alessandro a letter which spat out all the fury he felt in his heart, and the cardinal trembled as he read, 'You know well how much we have done for you, and with how much love. Never would we have believed how swiftly you were to forget our favours, and to set Orsino above ourselves. We beseech and exhort you not to repay us in such coin, since thus you do not satisfy those promises you so often gave us, much less your own honour and welfare.'

That same day, two other letters from Alexander arrived at

Capodimonte. The first was a ferocious and vindictive broadside aimed at Giulia. Under the Greek initials of Jesus Christ, Alexander wrote, 'Ungrateful and treacherous Giulia, we have received a letter of yours, by Navarico's hand, in which you signify and declare that your intention is not to come here unless Orsino wills it; and though hitherto we understood well enough both your wicked inclinations, and from whom you sought advice, nevertheless in consideration of your feigned and pretended assurances, we could not wholly persuade ourselves that you were capable of treating us with such ingratitude and disloyalty (having so often sworn and given your word to us that you were at our command, and would not keep company with Orsino) as now to do the contrary and go to Bassanello, at open peril of your life; nor can I believe that you are acting thus except to get yourself pregnant a second time by that horse of Bassanello. And we hope that very soon both you and Madame Adriana, most ungrateful of women, will acknowledge your fault and suffer condign punishment for it. And moreover, as regarding the present we command you, on pain of excommunication and eternal malediction, that you do not stir forth from Capodimonte, much less go to Bassanello for matters concerning our state.'

To Adriana, who had told Alexander they were running out of excuses for keeping Giulia at Capodimonte, he wrote, 'At last you have revealed all the evil and malice in your heart. Rest assured that you will suffer most condign punishment for your deceit.' Alexander ended by threatening Adriana with eternal damnation and confiscation of all her goods if she left Capodimonte without his permission. Cardinal Farnese also received a papal brief which expressly forbade Giulia from going to Bassanello, so that his advice to his sister could be tempered by church authority. And Alexander confided to his emissary at Capodimonte that he had decided to excommunicate both Giulia and Adriana if they persisted in their preference for 'that monkey', as he now described Orsino. To make sure that Orsino himself entertained no doubts about the seriousness of his pope, Alexander ordered an archdeacon to ride to Bassanello to inform the young man that if he did not appear in Rome within three days he too would face excommunication. A word of caution came to Alexander from Father Teseo Seripando, Orsino's adviser, who warned that if Giulia was snatched from him, anything might happen. For Orsino had become so enraged about his wife's love affair with Alexander that he was determined to keep her away from Rome, even if it meant his personal ruin. The warning fell on deaf ears.

Alexander also found separation from Lucrezia intolerable and wrote, urging her to come back to the safety of Rome. But his daughter also seemed in no hurry to rejoin him. If she was remiss in writing, Alexander was quick to complain, telling her on one occasion, 'For several days we have had no letter from you. Your neglect to write to us how you and Don Giovanni, our beloved son, are causes us great surprise. In the future be more heedful and diligent.' Sympathetically, Lucrezia responded, 'We understand that at present things are going badly in Rome...I implore Your Beatitude to leave and if that is not practical, to take the greatest possible care, and Your Beatitude must not impute this to presumption but to the very great love I bear and be certain, Your Holiness, that I will never be at peace unless I have frequent news of Your Holiness.'

The heavy-handed papal blackmail worked. Giulia and Andrea did not dare to go to Bassanello, and Orsino Orsini meekly rejoined his unit. Incredibly, once Alexander knew that Orsino was safely out of the way he lost interest in persuading the ladies to return to Rome. Both were relieved to be freed from the penal restrictions tying them to Capodimonte, and ventured out in late November 1494 to visit Cardinal Alessandro Farnese, who had recently been appointed Papal Legate to Viterbo, a town lying some miles to the north of Rome. On the way, they ran into advanced detachments of the French invading force, which just happened to be reconnoitring the road by which they were travelling. The astonished party was taken completely by surprise, and King Charles roared with laughter at this unexpected bonus falling to him. Ludovico Sforza cannily observed that the French had taken prisoner Alexander's 'heart and ears'.

The women were held for a ransom of three thousand gold ducats, and Alexander was informed of these terms. Shaken by the news, he immediately appointed an emissary to negotiate their release. Within days, an honorary guard of four hundred French cavalrymen escorted Adriana and Giulia into Rome, to the waiting pope. Alexander met them, as an observer recounted, 'arrayed in a black doublet bordered with gold brocade, with a beautiful belt in the Spanish fashion and with sword and dagger. He wore Spanish boots and a velvet biretta, all very gallant.' Alexander clearly wanted to look his best for the long-awaited reunion, and that night he and his young mistress slept together in his Vatican apartment.

Alexander was fiercely jealous of Giulia Farnese, but how faithful he remained to her is a matter of grave doubt. For Ludovico Sforza told the Milanese Senate that during the very week of his reunion with Giulia, he had slept with three other women – 'one of them being a nun of Valencia, the other a Castilian, a third a very beautiful girl from Venice, fifteen or sixteen years of age.' Ludovico was manifestly not a friend of the Borgias, and his quest for truth in matters concerning Alexander must have been, at best, highly suspect. Nevertheless, this provided further evidence for those who wanted to label the Borgias as the epitome of all things evil.

Soon afterwards Lucrezia was back in Rome, to the delight of her father. She rejoined Adriana del Mila and Giulia Farnese, whom she referred to as 'my mother and sister', at Santa Maria in Portico. Giovanni Sforza had responded to the pope's summons, and Alexander saw to it that he was sent off to command a brigade in the Neapolitan army. The appointment conflicted with his family loyalty to Ludovico Sforza, but he reconciled this by spying on Neapolitan army plans for the Milanese.

On December 19, 1494 Virginio Orsini, head of the Orsini

clan, captured the vital strategic fortress at Bracciano, a few miles from Rome and guarding the route to the city. Alexander realized resistance was pointless and that a battle in the streets would destroy the city, perhaps even costing him his throne. So he ordered King Alfonso to withdraw his troops and declared Rome an open city. This gave him and Cesare a few days' grace to seize all the valuables they could move from the Vatican into the Castel Sant'Angelo. Then they sat, waiting nervously in Alexander's ornate Vatican rooms for the French to arrive.

On New Year's Eve, King Charles led his army through the open gates of the Porta del Popolo. So long were his columns of armed men that the triumphal entry took six hours. Riding alongside Charles was Giuliano della Rovere, who had earlier fled to France to try to persuade the French king to hound Alexander from the papal throne. Della Rovere's motivation was purely personal – he wanted to be made pontiff himself. Other cardinals who supported della Rovere – his spies within the Sacred College – had been imprisoned by Alexander as security risks. Notable amongst these was Ascanio Sforza, who had switched allegiance on the orders of his cousin, Ludovico. In the cardinal's absence, his palace was looted by Neapolitan soldiers, enthusiastically aided by a Roman street mob.

To Alexander's distress, the crowds which turned out to view the French military procession cheered wildly, and he wondered if he should have taken King Alfonso's last-minute advice to abandon the city and head south with him. He had stayed because he feared, quite correctly, that della Rovere would take advantage of his absence to try to usurp the papal throne. Ludovico Sforza told an ambassador to his court that he was hourly awaiting, and looking forward to, the news that Alexander had been taken and beheaded.

In preparation for the unwelcome French visit to his city, Alexander had ordered a new defensive wall to be added to the Castel Sant'Angelo's fortifications. As Rome degenerated into a turmoil of looting and killing, Alexander led Cesare and five other cardinals along a secret, recently constructed underground passage leading from the Vatican to the security of the Castel. King Charles sent an emissary to demand that the stronghold be handed over, but Alexander refused, warning that if the Castel were attacked he would stand on the outer wall, a sitting target, but holding the most sacred relics of the church in his arms. Reluctant to risk heresy by damaging the relics, Charles installed himself and his immediate entourage across the Tiber in the Palazzo Venezia while he pondered how he was going to tackle the brave Alexander. Della Rovere urged Charles to call a council to depose the pope, but the king rejected this suggestion.

French cannons were lined up and aimed at the Castel Sant'Angelo but, before a shot could be fired, fate intervened as part of the fortress's stoutest defensive wall collapsed. Alexander realized that any further resistance was a waste of time and agreed to meet King Charles to discuss terms. On January 16 the youthful Charles, just twenty-four years old and not very intelligent, came face to face with the wily, sixty-three-year old pontiff at the Castel Sant' Angelo. As a matter of political expediency Charles had drawn up a proclamation calling for Alexander's deposition, but he tore this up when the pope readily agreed to hand out cardinal's hats to three of the king's advisers. Charles then acknowledged Alexander's papal authority, on condition that the pontiff gave an amnesty to those churchmen who had rebelled against him. The French army was also granted free passage through the Papal States while, as a guarantee of continued papal compliance, Cardinal Cesare Borgia was to accompany Charles as hostage. No mention was made of the Neapolitan succession, though Charles planned to raise this again later when his army had installed him as *de facto* monarch. Charles moved into a papal palace and made a public display of allegiance to Alexander which left della Rovere grinding his teeth.

It was a singular triumph for Alexander who, unarmed, could be said to have defeated the young king. For Charles had only obtained freedom of movement through the papal lands, which he had anyway, while Alexander had averted the threat to his throne by mesmerizing the young man with his courage.

The French army left Rome on January 28, 1495, but Cesare gave Charles the slip within a couple of days. Disguised as a stable boy, he made off in the middle of the night, leaving his cardinal's robe flung contemptuously across his bed. Charles was furious, and ordered the destruction of the nearest town in revenge. This order was only rescinded by the timely intervention of Cardinal della Rovere, a willing and protected companion of the journey south. Cesare made his way to Spoleto where he took refuge while Charles fumed. Alexander was quick to apologize on his son's behalf, but denied any knowledge of Cesare's flight. Charles was unimpressed by this, and raged, 'All Italians are dirty dogs, and the Holy Father is as bad as the worst of them!' His anger was justified, for Alexander and Cesare had in fact planned the escape down to the last detail before the party had left Rome. In an account of the incident Johannes Burchard recorded, 'In his departure from Rome with King Charles, he had arranged for nineteen mules to follow him, laden with his goods and wearing rich trappings; amongst them were two beasts carrying chests with all his valuables. On the first day out, however, when His Majesty and the cardinals were still on their way to Marino, these beasts had remained behind and returned to the city in the evening, whilst the cardinal's servants made the excuse at the king's court that the mules had been stolen by some bandits.'

The daring Cesare was back in Rome by the beginning of April, when he heard that a detachment of Swiss mercenaries left behind by King Charles had plundered and wrecked his mother's town house. He gathered together two thousand Spaniards to ambush and kill twenty-four Swiss in the Piazza San Pietro. It was a ruthless, savage revenge and displayed a facet of Cesare's nature which potential enemies learned to fear.

Cesare's presence had, however, proved unnecessary to the French army, which continued its parade south for an easy conquest of Naples. King Alfonso did not relish the prospect of capture by the mighty French army, so he declared a cowardly abdication of the throne in favour of his son Ferrantino, and sailed to Sicily. Neapolitan resistance crumbled and within days Ferrantine was following his father into exile, accompanied by his court, including Jofre Borgia and Princess Sancia.

Naples seemed an earthly paradise to the men of the French army, with its warm climate and beautiful women. At first the Neapolitans welcomed the French as liberators who were freeing them from the hated Aragon yoke. But when the troops started looting homes and raping the women, the local people realized they had merely exchanged one set of fiendish rulers for another. The French troops started falling ill with syphilis, a then-unknown and deadly disease which they called 'the sickness of Naples'. The Neapolitans, on the other hand, believed the invaders had brought the illness with them and called it 'the French disease'.

Charles offered Alexander a bribe of one hundred and fifty thousand gold ducats, to be followed by a large yearly tribute, for his papal investiture as king of Naples. This was rejected, but Charles nevertheless dressed himself in imperial clothes and crown for a mock coronation.

Then news reached him that Alexander had contrived to set up an anti-French alliance between the papacy, Venice, Milan, Spain and the Holy Roman Empire, known as the Holy League. The Milanese and Venetians had been persuaded to join after the spectacular success of the French. Ludovico Sforza had wanted to weaken the Neapolitans, not destroy them. Now he, in common with the other rulers of the League states, was worried that the triumphant French might try to defeat the other Italian domains, including his own, one by one. Charles decided to abandon his plans for a crusade, and to return to France before the forces of the League cut off his retreat. He left several garrisons behind in a half-hearted attempt to hold Naples, but these men were doomed to be killed either by Neapolitans seeking revenge or massacred by the forces of the Holy League.

As Charles retraced his steps, he still entertained hopes of forcing the investiture from Alexander. He stopped at Rome, only to find that the pope, reading the king's mind, had left for Orvieto to avoid him. Alexander had also sent Lucrezia, Adriana del Mila and Giulia Farnese out of town to avoid any unwelcome attention the rapacious French troops might have planned for them. Charles followed Alexander to Orvieto, only to find that he had moved on to the papal fortress at Perugia. The king still wanted his investiture, but not enough to risk being trapped by the Holy League army which his intelligence sources told him was gathering to greet the retreating French in northern Italy. So he marched his troops as fast as they could move along the roads they had covered so easily just a few months before.

On July 5, 1495 Charles met the forces which the Holy League had managed to muster at Fornovo in a bloody but inconclusive battle. Most of his army survived, but he lost all the booty he had plundered from Naples, and limped home to France. On the same day, King Ferrantino retook Naples while Alexander, Charles's jubilant adversary in Rome, had almost effortlessly weathered the storm to emerge stronger than ever.

6

A DEATH IN THE FAMILY

The last French garrisons in Naples were overwhelmed by Holy League forces, led by the formidable Spanish 'Great Captain', Gonsalvo di Cordova. Among his troops was the feckless Giovanni Sforza, Lucrezia Borgia's husband, who had finally and reluctantly taken an active part in the campaign. Among his prisoners was Virginio Orsini, head of the Orsini family, who had been captured in Naples and incarcerated in the city's grim Castel del Uova on instructions from Alexander. Virginio died there shortly after, and his death served to exacerbate the vendetta between the Borgias and the Orsinis.

With the French threat behind him – apart from their continued occupation of the fortress at Ostia – Alexander decided it was time he dealt a lethal blow to the Orsinis, whom he regarded as vipers in the papal bed. The Roman barons had shown themselves totally unreliable, and Alexander's thoughts turned to the undoubted strength of family allegiance. However, his favouritism for his son Juan, second Duke of Gandia, marred Alexander's normally faultless judgement.

Juan, now aged twenty, had settled comfortably into his role as a feudal duke in Spain, dividing his time between ceremonial duties on behalf of King Ferdinand and the pleasures of hunting. His life resembled that of a decadent monarch, and he developed a relentless arrogance which caused a contemporary observer to assess him as 'a very mean young man, full of false ideas of grandeur and bad thoughts, haughty, cruel, and unreasonable.'

If Alexander was aware of his son's reputation, he ignored

it. He also evaded the obvious truth that Juan could claim no military experience, and had distinguished himself only as a prolific lover of women, gambling and fine clothes. A papal directive ordered the young man to leave his pregnant wife and his son in Gandia while he reported to family headquarters in Rome to receive an assignment of the highest significance.

Juan entered Rome in August 1496 like an eastern potentate, dressed in a velvet coat and cap studded with precious stones and pearls, a flowing Turkish robe and mounted on a horse draped in a gold cloth hung with tinkling bells. It was a dazzling moment, which made a strong impression on many Renaissance chroniclers. Alexander welcomed his favourite son with open arms at the Vatican, and took him inside for a family reunion. The Borgias had converged on Rome in force that summer – the Godfather pope wanted his children around him while outstanding family business was being resolved.

Cesare had been given a suite of rooms directly above Alexander's own apartment so that he would always be available as *consigliere*. He had become fascinated by war and the associated politics of intrigue after watching at close hand as the pope outwitted the young French king to turn a potential disaster into a triumph. We can only guess at the jealousy Cesare must have felt for his younger brother, their father's pride and joy, as he pondered the future in the colourful and flamboyant Vatican rooms which so aptly reflected the Borgia character. Lucrezia, who had kept clear of any unwelcome French attention at the homely and uneventful court of Pesaro, was staying at the Vatican annexe of Santa Maria in Portico. With her was Giulia Farnese, still Alexander's mistress.

Jofre Borgia and Princess Sancia needed twenty-eight mules to carry the baggage they brought with them from Naples. So many cardinals, ambassadors, senators, Vatican soldiers and noblemen turned out to greet the couple that their entry to Rome became a procession. Alexander and Cesare peeked out upon the scene through half-open shutters at the Vatican. Like most of the other observers, they were stunned at the incongruity of the ravishing Sancia alongside the boyish innocence of Jofre. It explained to the pope the reasons behind the lascivious tales which had been passed on to him from the Neapolitan court. Soon Rome too was bubbling with stories about Sancia which claimed that, bored with the physical attributes of her youthful husband, she had entertained both Cesare and Juan in her bed.

Alexander spent the next weeks openly and joyously among his family, without a trace of diplomatic pretence about whose children they were. News of the papal boldness reached the Florentine preacher Savonarola, who declared, 'Once annointed priests called their sons nephews, but now they speak no more of their nephews, but always and everywhere of their sons.'

Lucrezia struck up an instant friendship with the vivacious Princess Sancia. Each was attracted by the sparkle in the other's personality. They showed a joint irreverence for solemn church occasions when they attended a service in St Peter's in the company of Alexander. Bored with an overlong and tedious sermon, they climbed to the choir reserved for canons and sat on the marble stand from which the gospel was read, chattering and laughing loudly.

By late October, Alexander's plans to break the Orsini power once and for all were complete. Juan Borgia, wearing boots and spurs, was the centrepiece of another Vatican ceremony when his father installed him as Captain-General of the Church. The very next day, the young man led the holy forces out of Rome. Cardinal Lunate was appointed Legate, 'to assist in reducing the lands of the Orsini to papal obedience.' The renowned *condotierre*, Guidobaldo da Montefeltre, Duke of Urbino, rode alongside Juan, nominally his second-in-command but in fact there to give the campaign the military brain so conspicuously lacking in its leader.

The nobles of Rome, who would normally have expected the Captain-General's job to go to one of their better-qualified number, were aghast at Alexander's choice. They regarded Juan as an upstart, the incompetent son of a doting pope. His offensively arrogant manner since returning to Rome had done nothing to alter their opinion or to endear Juan to his contemporaries.

Despite such an inauspicious opening to Juan's military career, the punitive war against the Orsini began on a highly successful note. Within a month, ten of the family's castles had been taken, and Alexander looked forward to the pleasure of taking revenge on his long-standing enemies.

However, Juan's fortunes changed dramatically at Bracciano, the main Orsini stronghold which had been handed to the French, opening their way to Rome during the invasion. The Orsini defiance of papal authority was expressed by the French flags still fluttering from the five battlemented round towers. A resolute defence was led by Bartolomea Orsini, Virginio's brother, and assault after assault was repulsed. It was a bloody battle, fought in the muddy terrain of the rainy season, and papal losses were high. The Duke of Urbino was injured during one attack, and command of the force fell to the incompetent Juan Borgia. He decided to try to bribe defenders out of the fortress by offering them higher pay. Bartolomea Orsini responded to this by sending a donkey out of the castle gates with a placard round its neck reading, 'Let me come through, in me you see an ambassador to the Duke of Gandia.' Attached to the donkey's tail was an insulting letter addressed to Juan. Seething with anger, he threw more men into the attack, only to see many of them die before the stout walls of Bracciano.

When word reached Juan of the approach of an army raised by French money and commanded by one of Virginio Orsini's sons, he broke off the siege to meet the new threat. His incompetence led his troops into a trap on unfavourable ground in a narrow valley. The men under his command fought valiantly, but it was hopeless. They were defeated after a bloody battle, the Duke of Urbino was captured, and an injured Juan limped back to Rome with the remnants of his force to give Alexander his own self-serving account of the fighting. At first Alexander wanted to continue the now hopeless struggle to tame the Orsini, so intent was he on seeking glory for the inept Juan. But he finally settled for a compromise peace. All the captured castles were handed back to the Orsini, restoring their power, while the family agreed to pay the papacy fifty thousand gold ducats for them. Most of this money Alexander gave to Juan as a kind of consolation prize.

Blind to Juan's defects, the indulgent Alexander promptly appointed him to lead another military expedition. This time the aim was more modest: to dislodge the French from the mighty fortress at Ostia, which had been used to interrupt Rome's flow of supplies. Gonsalvo di Cordova, fresh from military operations in Naples, was conscripted to serve as Juan's lieutenant. After a siege and an attack, both master-minded by di Cordova, the fortress and its defenders were captured, and Juan returned to Rome in triumph. Alexander knew the outcome of this particular assault was inevitable, and had schemed it to allow his son some glory. Less happy was the acknowledged military leader, di Cordova. Because Juan was given the place of honour at the subsequent cele-brations, di Cordova refused to take his seat. This enmity was noted by the Roman families, who could well under-stand di Cordova's feelings.

Alexander was aware of people's hostility, but attributed it to jealousy of Juan. His abiding commitment was still to build up and consolidate family power, and he devoted all his attentions to this. He increased his control over the Sacred College by appointing four new Spanish cardinals, including another nephew who was also named Juan Borgia. Then he began to examine greater possibilities.

Naples held a fascination for him similar to the spell it had cast on the covetous Charles VIII. The state was weak enough, Alexander considered, for a powerful family to move in to take over the royal line. When King Ferrantino died suddenly and without children in December 1496, Alex-ander believed there was an opportunity for him and for his chosen son, Juan Borgia. He toyed with the idea of investing Juan as the new king, since Naples was still nominally a papal fief, and facing the consequences. However, word of this outrageous scheme reached the court of King Ferdinand in Aragon, who was quick to warn Alexander that he would in no way countenance such a change of dynasty, and would, if necessary, go to war to keep his family on the throne. Alexander realized his gambit would never succeed in the face of such powerful opposition. Submitting to the Spanish lord, he acknowledged Ferrantino's uncle Federigo as the legitimate successor.

Juan Borgia was already a prince of Naples and feudal lord of small territories there as a result of earlier negotiations over Jofre's marriage to Sancia. Alexander now expanded the young man's power and influence in the kingdom by joining the papal cities within the Neapolitan boundaries – Benvento, Terracina, and Pontecorvo – into a hereditary dukedom for Juan. A murmur of protest swept Rome at this move, which was announced in early June 1497. Shrewd observers realized that Alexander was planning a takeover of Naples by stealth, using this dukedom as the first wedge. With Naples and the Papal States under Borgia control, what would there be to stop Alexander's family power growing until they exercised control over all of Italy? Those who reasoned in this way had correctly assessed Alexander's intentions.

To celebrate her pride in her son's elevation in life, Vannozza de' Cattanei gave a dinner at her country home set in a vineyard. It was a select family gathering with Juan, his brothers Cesare and Jofre, his sister-in-law Princess Sancia, and their cousin Cardinal Juan Borgia-Lanzol. Towards the end of the dinner a masked man, who had frequently been seen in Juan's company at the Vatican, came to whisper something to Juan, then retired to wait for him outside. The party broke up as dusk gathered, for the guests wanted to be sure to get home before dark, when wealthy travellers were prey to the night marauders of Rome. Juan rode to Trastevere with Cesare, then, telling his brother he was going 'in search of further pleasure', rode off with the masked man and a groom. The trio went to the Piazza degli Ebrei, where Juan told the groom to wait one hour for him. If he was not back in that time, the groom was free to go home. He rode away with the masked man – and was never seen alive again.

When Juan failed to come home next morning, Cesare told their father what he knew. Both agreed that Juan must have gone off for a secret assignation with a lady, and tried not to worry about his absence. Alexander said that the young man was probably waiting till nightfall, so as not to compromise the lady's reputation by being seen leaving her home.

By that evening, such consoling thoughts were no longer possible, and Alexander ordered an inch-by-inch search of the city. The groom who had waited for Juan was discovered, so badly beaten that he was close to death and unable to say what had happened. Juan's horse was found, and its damaged stirrups bore mute testimony to a ferocious struggle. There was still no sign of Juan, and Spanish cohorts of the Borgias terrorized the population as they conducted a frantic search for him. Many Romans, particularly members of the Orsini and Colonna families, barricaded themselves in their homes to avoid the more enthusiastic attentions of the searchers.

Eventually a witness was found. Giorgio Schiavi was a timber merchant who had unloaded his wood near the ancient hospital of San Girolama del Schiavoni, set on an island in the middle of the Tiber, and he had kept watch on his property throughout the night of Juan's disappearance. He recounted, 'That night about the hour of two, while I was guarding my wood, lying in my boat, two men on foot came out of the alley on the left of the Ospedale degli Schiavoni, onto the open way by the river. They looked cautiously about them to see that no one was passing, and not having found anyone, returned the way they had come into the same alley. Shortly afterwards, two other men came out of the same alley, also looking furtively round them; not seeing anybody, they made a signal to their companions. Then there appeared a rider on a white horse, carrying a body slung across its crupper behind him, the head and arms hanging to one side, the legs to the other, supported on the right by the two first men so that it should not fall off. Having reached the point from which refuse is thrown into the river, the horseman turned his horse so that its tail faced the river, then the two men who were standing on either side, taking the body, one by the hands and arms, the other by the feet and legs, flung it with all their strength into the river. To the horseman's demand whether the body had sunk, they replied, "Yes, sir", then the horseman looked again at the river and saw the dead man's cloak floating on the water, and asked what it was. They answered, "Sir, the cloak". Then he threw some stones at it and made it sink. This done, all five, including the other two who had come out of the alley to keep watch, went away by an alley which leads to the Ospedale di San Giacomo.'

Alexander's investigators asked Signor Schiavi why he had not reported the incident to the authorities. The simple answer was a telling indication of the value placed on life in the turbulent city: 'In the course of my life, on various nights, I have seen more that a hundred bodies thrown into the river right at this spot, and never heard of anyone troubling himself about them.'

A reward was offered for the finder of Juan's body, and three hundred fishermen and boatmen started dragging the Tiber. Within hours, a body dressed in brocade bearing the insignia of Captain-General of the Church was hauled up in a fisherman's net, at a point close to the church of Santa Maria del Popolo, and opposite the garden of a small villa owned by Cardinal Ascanio Sforza. It was Juan Borgia. He had been stabbed eight times, his throat cut, his hands roped together, and a stone tied to his neck to submerge the body. He was still fully dressed, and his gloves were tucked into a belt which contained thirty gold coins, evidence that the motive for his death had not been robbery.

The muddy and bloated corpse was taken by boat to the Castel Sant'Angelo and when Alexander saw what had happened to his son he let out a roar like a wounded animal that was clearly audible to people outside the walls. Johannes Burchard described Alexander's distress in his diary: 'The pope, when he heard that the duke had been killed and flung into the river like dung, was thrown into a paroxysm of grief, and for the pain and bitterness of his heart shut himself in his room and wept most bitterly. The Cardinal of Segovia and some of his servants went to the door, persuading him to open it, which he did only after many hours. The pope neither ate nor drank anything from the Wednesday evening until the following Saturday, nor from the morning of Thursday to the following Sunday did he know a moment's peace. At last, however, after being exhorted by friends, His Holiness agreed to begin ending his mourning insofar as he was able, since he understood that otherwise he would bring greater harm and danger to himself through it.'

Juan Borgia was buried in the evening of the day on which his body was found. A procession led by one hundred and twenty torch-bearers wound its path, amidst much weeping and wailing, from the Vatican to his family chapel, prepared by Vannozza de' Cattanei, at Santa Maria del Popolo. As the cortege passed the spot where the body had been recovered from the Tiber, the Borgia men-at-arms unsheathed their swords and swore a vendetta against whoever had perpetrated the crime. Burchard described the scene in the church: 'The body was borne in a magnificent bier so that all could see it, and it seemed that the duke was not dead, but sleeping.'

The murder of his favourite son – 'the hope and glory of his lines', as contemporaries referred to Juan – was the greatest tragedy of Alexander's life. He emerged from his traumatic seclusion to address cardinals and ambassadors gathered for a Church Council: 'The Duke of Gandia is dead. His death has given us the greatest sorrow, and no greater pain than this could we suffer, because we loved him above all things, and esteemed not more the papacy nor anything else. Rather, had we seven papacies we would give them all to have the duke alive again.'

Alexander was convinced his son's horrific death was a divine retribution for the error of his ways. He told the Council: 'God has done this, perhaps, for some sin of ours, and not because he deserved such a cruel death. Nor do we know who killed him and threw him into the Tiber. May God forgive whoever committed the crime.'

Plagued with an overbearing sense of guilt, for it was he who had ordered Juan back to Rome from Spain, Alexander pledged himself to seeking God's good graces through reform of the church and his family's role in it. He promised, 'We are determined from henceforth to see to our own reform, and that of the church. We wish to renounce all nepotism. We will begin therefore with ourselves and so proceed through all the ranks of the church till the whole work is accomplished.'

In an attempt to purge his guilt, Alexander set up a commission consisting of six cardinals to examine abuses of the church government. He ordered Jofre Borgia and Princess Sancia to return to Naples, while he announced that he wanted Lucrezia to go to live in Spain. Plans were laid for various reforms, and he promised to discuss them with the Sacred College.

It seemed that Alexander was determined to rid the Vatican of the sinister presence of his many relatives, but these plans, along with the others, were prompted by grief, and when the first wave of sadness passed he abandoned them. Political circumstances made it impossible for him to keep firm control without numerous relatives judiciously holding key posts. Even while the same council was in session, he showed that he could not change the habits of a lifetime.

In the official announcement of Juan's death, Alexander declared that he did not know 'by whom the murder had been committed or what had been its cause.' This was doubtless true, but there was no shortage of suspects, for the numbers of Borgia-haters were ever increasing. Juan's movements on the night of his death were never established, though he was believed to have spent his last hours in the arms of a woman. One account suggested she was Madonna Damiata, a notorious Roman courtesan, another that Juan had been lured to his death by the promise of the beautiful and virtuous daughter of a Roman nobleman, with whom he had fallen desperately in love. This would have accounted for the mysterious presence of the masked man, whose identity was never established.

It was also suggested that the man behind the killing was Jofre Borgia, motivated by hatred because he had found out that his brother Juan was having an affair with his wife. Giovanni Sforza was suspected as well, because of the bad feeling between him and Alexander over Lucrezia, and so was Cardinal Ascanio Sforza because Juan's body was discovered near his villa. One group of Borgia supporters were so convinced of his guilt that they ransacked his palace. To clear the air, Alexander suggested a meeting with Ascanio, but the cardinal agreed to a confrontation only if it took place in the company of a vast array of diplomats. When it was over, he fled from Rome to hide. The military commanders, the Duke of Urbino and Gonsalvo di Cordova, were also paraded as suspects, angry at being forcibly suborned to the inept Juan.

Alexander publicly informed the Church Council that he did not consider any of these suspects to be responsible for the crime. But there was another group with the deadliest motive of all, who had been freely suggested as the culprits and whom Alexander pointedly did not absolve. They were the Orsini family. Their motive was the family feud which had been raging between them and the Borgias since the time of Pope Calixtus. The Orsini also blamed Alexander for the death of Virginio Orsini in prison – his body had been brought through Rome en route for burial at Bracciano less than two months before Juan's death. What better way could there be to strike back at Alexander than to kill his favourite son?

Within three weeks of Juan's death, Alexander ordered the investigation closed, and it was never reopened. This convinced observers that the pope knew who the murderers were, or at least who had hired them. Alexander was later to confide that he knew who had committed the murder, but refrained from taking his revenge because he wanted to avoid a civil war in the Romagna. The Milanese ambassador to

Rome later informed Ludovico Sforza, now the duke: 'Evidence linking the Orsini to the crime has been uncovered, but the more it got verified, the more careful the pope became not to let the matter be known before the right time.' Another ambassador reported that the pope had 'acquired the certainty that the Orsini had murdered the duke'. And yet another was to write, 'It seems that His Holiness declares himself more openly than before in accusing the Orsini of having killed the Duke of Gandia.'

Juan Borgia, it is almost certain, was the victim of a contract killing. The motives and circumstantial evidence convinced Alexander that the Orsinis were behind it. He was determined to avenge the death, but he was in no hurry. He would wait until the opportunity arose. Meanwhile Cesare Borgia's name belatedly entered the list of suspects, as it became clear that he, more than anyone else, would benefit from his brother's death. The accusation was whispered around Rome's diplomatic circuit and reached the ears of Niccolo Machiavelli, the Florentine statesman, whose devious mind added a macabre, incestuous motivation. Cesare had set up the murder of Juan, he claimed, through envy or jealousy over Madonna Lucrezia'. Though unsupported by fact, this story was repeated over the years, and has been passed down the centuries. The truth is that there is not, and never was, any evidence to link Cesare with the crime.

7

LUCREZIA CHANGES PARTNERS

Giovanni Sforza had been a consistently disappointing son-in-law to Alexander. His reluctant obedience to papal and family authority was a constant annoyance. The family link with Milan, instead of bringing the Borgias support in the Italian political turmoil, had turned into a counter-productive embarrassment, as Ludovico Sforza became a willing accomplice to French designs on Naples. The split loyalty this provoked in Giovanni made him a very suspect character to have within the Vatican circle. For Alexander was a man who demanded total obedience from those who hoped to benefit from association with him.

Even when the Milanese-French link was broken with the formation of the Holy League, Giovanni had not been anxious to serve as a pro-papal commander. Alexander wanted his son-in-law to serve in the operations which cleared away the garrisons remaining after the exit of the main French force, but Giovanni was very reluctant. Finally, Alexander threatened Giovanni while cloaking it as an appeal to his conscience, and wrote to him, 'We are surprised that when the Duke of Urbino and others who are not as closely tied to us as your lordship come to serve us of their own free will, you refuse to do so. Wherever you may find yourself in receipt of this letter, we exhort you to come to us, bringing as many soldiers as you have.' This worked, and Giovanni took the men under his command to Naples, but he was still a most unenthusiastic soldier.

When the Neapolitan campaign ended, Giovanni did not return to his wife's side in Rome, but travelled on to Pesaro, where he could feel master in his own house. Once again, a papal edict was delivered to Giovanni, ordering him to go to the Borgia headquarters. Lucrezia, bemused by the family politicking going on around her, showed her delight when Giovanni came back to Rome in January 1497. She was, according to one observer, 'very happy and quite mad about her husband'. This description seems a little exaggerated, for Lucrezia's marriage was never more than emotionally tepid, and it had taken the force of a papal directive to encourage her husband back to her side. But it did at least save Lucrezia the embarrassment of appearing a rejected wife.

For Giovanni, the next months were tense and unhappy. He felt smothered by the papal court and subjected to intolerable family pressures, which were increased when Juan Borgia returned from Spain. It was a Borgia world in which he played no great part. His every move was monitored, and decisions were dictated by the transient whim of Alexander.

The young husband was painfully aware that the Sforza link was now something of an imposition on the Borgias. He repeatedly asked Alexander for permission to take Lucrezia back to his home in Pesaro, as the marriage contract specified he was entitled to do. His requests were always ignored. Then he heard that the Borgias were reconsidering the wisdom of matching their daughter to an obscure provincial baron, and that Alexander believed his daughter had been wasted on him. They might have matched her higher, he heard, and the possibility of marrying her into the ruling Aragonese family of Naples was mentioned. Giovanni realized it would be difficult for the Borgias to free Lucrezia from him, given the rigid constrictions of the church on divorce. In any event, no royal family would want to accept a woman sullied by a previous marriage and the consequent implied loss of virginity. Lucrezia and Giovanni had lived apart for much of their marriage, but the time they had spent sleeping under the same roof meant that it would be difficult to persuade a church court that their union had not been consummated. Royal brides had at least to have a veneer of virginity, even if the reality was something very different.

But Giovanni's nervousness turned to panic when he

heard rumours of a plan being concocted by Alexander and Cesare which would overcome such an obstacle. Widows were considered respectable, for the death of their husbands was viewed as an act of God. The Borgias were scheming to poison him, he was told, to clear the way for a new and more beneficial match. One account tells of a chamberlain overhearing Cesare discussing the plot with Lucrezia, and passing the information on to the prospective victim.

Giovanni rose early on the first morning of Holy Week in March 1497 and told Lucrezia he was going to confession. He mounted his horse, but instead of riding to church he headed out of Rome and along the road to Pesaro. He did not stop till he arrived, exhausted, in his home town that night.

Alexander was furious when he heard that the family captive had flown from his gilded Vatican cage. Now he would have to engineer the marriage break-up without being able to put pressure on Giovanni from close quarters. Giovanni, for his part, wanted to keep his wife and the valuable dowry which had come with her. He knew divorce would mean that he had to relinquish the money, but he had already spent it. He wrote to Lucrezia, asking her to quit the oppressive papal circle and go to Pesaro to be with him. It was an open defiance of the clearly-expressed papal wishes of Alexander. The pope was not about to let his daughter out of his care again, and even if Lucrezia had wanted to go to Pesaro, it would have been impossible, for she would not have been provided with the escort essential to the hazardous cross-country journey. This problem did not arise, however, because Lucrezia was more than content to remain close to her father.

Within days of Giovanni's precipitous flight, Alexander's special messenger arrived in Pesaro with a letter for him. In a plea interwoven with a threat, Alexander wrote, 'Your own good judgement can tell you how deeply grieved we are by your unexpected departure from the city; and since in our opinion there is no other remedy for an act of this nature, if you wish to safeguard your honour, we exhort you most strongly to return here as soon as possible.' Giovanni responded by demanding that his wife be sent to him. Alexander met this firmly by informing Giovanni that if he did not return to Rome as ordered, he would never set eyes on Lucrezia again.

Alexander and his Vatican advisers pored over the church law books, searching for a way to end this now most undesirable marriage. Papal lawyers told Alexander that, while they sympathized with his position and fully understood his desire to be rid of an unreliable son-in-law, the obstacles placed in the way of a divorce by church regulations were formidable. Alexander retorted that his long service as Vice-Chancellor had given him a close view of all the obstacles. Their task, if the advisers wanted to keep their valuable posts, was to find a way round them.

Their investigations led the lawyers to the reluctant conclusion that the only possible grounds for divorce would be that the marriage had never been consummated. If this were established, the church could take the view that the marriage had never happened. However, there were obvious problems, for the union had existed for four years. To put the issue beyond doubt, therefore, it was essential to have a declaration from Giovanni Sforza admitting that, because of impotence, he had never had sexual intercourse with his wife. A second, less likely, possibility was put forward: the marriage might be declared invalid on the grounds that Lucrezia had never been legally freed from her commitment to marry her Spanish suitor, Don Gasparo de Procida. Alexander's church lawyers impressed upon him that a Vatican court would be very likely to reject this second option, though Giovanni might find it eminently more palatable.

Accordingly, two writs for divorce were drawn up. The first claimed the marriage had never been consummated, the second that it was invalidated by Lucrezia's prior betrothal to Don Gasparo. On May 26, 1497 Father Mariano da Genazzano, the able lawyer Alexander had put in charge of the case, took the writs to Giovanni in Pesaro. He explained carefully that the young man was faced with two alternatives. Giovanni could confess that he had never been able to have sexual intercourse with his wife because of his own impotence, or he could agree to an annulment on the grounds that Lucrezia had never been clear of her earlier commitment.

Father da Genazzano was aware that the second alternative would never get past a church court. But he hoped that if he could persuade Giovanni to accept it as the lesser of two evils, it might be possible later to induce him to accept a declaration of impotence, no matter how unsavoury it might have initially appeared to him. The papal emissary informed Giovanni that he could take seven days to consider.

Now it was Giovanni's turn to explode. For an Italian man of the Renaissance, the idea of admitting to being impotent was horrifying. He was not about to have himself publicly emasculated, and made it clear to Alexander that he would battle to preserve his honour. Searching for support, he hurried to Milan to beg for backing from his cousin Ludovico Sforza, Duke of Milan. Giovanni described to him the sex life he had shared with Lucrezia, which belied the suggestion that the marriage had never been consummated. Ludovico listened sympathetically and urged the young man to prove his virility beyond any shadow of a doubt in order to make the charge of impotence ridiculous. He told Giovanni to ask the pope to send Lucrezia to a neutral location where, in the presence of mutually acceptable witnesses, he could demonstrate his masculinity with his wife. If he was averse to putting Lucrezia through the humiliation of such a public demonstration, then Ludovico suggested that he could prove his virility with prostitutes in a brothel, and have the spectacle witnessed by the Papal Legate to Milan, Alexander's nephew, Juan Borgia-Lanzol. Ludovico pointed out that, coarse as the proposed exhibition might seem, many men had undergone such a potency test.

Ludovico listened to Giovanni but made it abundantly plain that, beyond giving advice, he was not prepared to put any pressure on Alexander over the proposed divorce, upon which he could already see the pope was absolutely determined. The papacy, aided by Alexander's astute power broking, was more powerful than it had been for centuries, and Ludovico was not prepared to risk the temporal wrath of Alexander's allies in the cause of a cousin who was unimportant in his own scheme of things. He did, however, persuade Giovanni to write to the papal commission which was examining the case to ask for his marriage to be annulled on the grounds that Lucrezia had always been bound by her betrothal to the jilted Spanish fiancé. Ludovico saw this as a possible way out of the dilemma (Alexander had latched onto the proposal for the same reason). But their hopes were dashed by the eminent church jurist, Cardinal Antonio San Giorgio, who brushed the compromise aside, declaring that the grounds were 'neither just nor honest, nor in accord with the law'. San Giorgio pointed out that if, after the years Lucrezia had lived with Giovanni, she was still 'without nuptial intercourse and carnal knowledge', and that if she was prepared to swear to this and submit herself to the examination of an obstetrician, it would be possible for the commission to order a divorce on these grounds. However, to be absolutely certain of the outcome, Giovanni would have to signify agreement by declaring his impotence.

The proposition was put to Giovanni once again, but he asserted that nothing could induce him to sign such a declaration. He said, 'I would prefer to lose my estate and my life itself rather than my honour.'

Giovanni then appealed to Cardinal Ascanio Sforza, the cousin he hoped might be able to influence Alexander in his position as Vice-Chancellor. He wrote, 'I do not want to agree to this dissolution, for no man under God could do so, and even were I to give my consent it would be invalid owing to the things that have passed between me and the said Madonna Lucrezia, as I explained at greater length to His Excellency the most illustrious Lord Duke things that I do not care to repeat here, and that I shall not repeat unless I am obliged to.'

When Alexander then put pressure on Ludovico to persuade Giovanni to make the declaration, the young husband felt trapped. Giovanni told Ludovico that he had had sexual intercourse with Lucrezia 'an infinite number of times'. This made no difference to Ludovico, who had never entertained any doubts about the matter, and he again told Giovanni that he would have to find some way to comply with the pope's wishes.

In desperation, Giovanni lashed out at his papal tormentor. He had always felt in competition with Alexander for Lucrezia's love, and his resentment and frustration combined to produce a vitriolic (though false) accusation which has nevertheless been passed down to us. The pope, Giovanni told Ludovico, was trying to get rid of him 'because he wanted his daughter for himself', and 'he had known her carnally on countless occasions'. This accusation was picked up by ambassadorial gossipers and snowballed until Lucrezia was reputed to be giving her favours not only to Alexander, but also to her brothers Juan and Cesare. Giovanni threatened to broadcast his allegations if the pressure on him to admit impotence was not lifted. Alexander responded by spreading stories of Giovanni's impotence, even though it was well known that Giovanni's first wife had died in childbirth, and that he had fathered at least one illegitimate daughter.

That he was making his own daughter a laughing stock does not seem to have bothered Alexander, but Lucrezia was disturbed by the scandal surrounding her marriage. She had believed in the lasting sanctity of marriage, and had taken seriously the vows she swore in the Vatican ceremony. That her father should now ask her to break those vows perplexed her. She was also frightened at the prospect of a court case to establish the non-consummation of her union with Giovanni. For this could mean testifying that she was still a virgin when an examination by a midwife might reveal that this was not true. So, shortly after her husband fled from Rome, Lucrezia left Santa Maria in Portico to take up residence in the San Sisto Convent a few miles away on the Via Appia. She had decided to lock herself away from the world while the divorce battle was resolved. If there was no solution, she would consider committing herself to the discipline and authority of one even mightier than her father.

The murder of his son Juan, Duke of Gandia, brought Alexander's plotting to a halt, but not for long. Stricken by remorse, he denounced the corruption of the church to a specially-called council. However, this did not stop him raising the question of Lucrezia's divorce before the same council. The marriage, he averred, had not been consummated because of Giovanni's impotence. The annulment asked for, he said, was to end an incomplete union and would be an act of righteousness. He was lying, and he well knew it, yet this did not deter him.

Alexander and Cesare made it clear to Cardinal Ascanio Sforza that neither of them would rest until Lucrezia was divorced from Giovanni. Their consciences, they said, would not allow them to leave her in the hands of such a man. The cardinal wrote to Ludovico Sforza, spelling out that Alexander 'would have liked this marriage to be a lasting one', but realized it had to be ended since 'it had remained unconsummated as a result of impotence'. The pope, he said, would do anything to extract a signed confession of impotence from Giovanni.

Both Ludovico and his cardinal cousin realized they would have to force Giovanni's hand if they wanted to keep Alexander's friendship. Alexander had meanwhile come to the conclusion that the main obstacle to Giovanni's compliance was his fear that he would lose Lucrezia's dowry. So the pope let Giovanni know, in a message delivered by a top secret courier, that he could keep the money in exchange for the required confession. Still Giovanni held out, until Ludovico warned that he would withdraw his protection, sugaring the threat by letting him know that a new marriage was being arranged for him. Giovanni finally decided to give in, but he told Ludovico, 'If His Holiness wishes to establish his own kind of justice, I cannot gainsay him. Let him do what he wishes, for God is higher.'

Lucrezia was brought from the convent to her father in the Vatican. He told her the divorce must go through, and that

118

she would be obliged to swear to her virginity before the papal commission. Any reservations she may have had were presumably overcome by Alexander's obvious determination. He assured her that he would find another suitable young man for her, and that he always had her welfare in mind. But she knew her father's main concern was fulfilling his own dynastic ambitions, and that there was little she could do to influence him. Accordingly, she agreed to appear before the commission to describe her marriage. She told the truth when she said she had never been in love with her husband. She lied when she said there had never been any sex between them.

On November 18, 1497, Giovanni, feeling humiliated and defeated, appeared before the same commission to sign a spurious confession that his impotence had precluded intercourse with Lucrezia. A month later their divorce was announced by the Vatican, and the commission declared Lucrezia to be *virga intacta*. The way was thus opened for another marriage when a suitably important candidate could be found by her family. The commission's pronouncement provoked hoots of derision. As one chronicler noted, it was 'a conclusion that set all Italy laughing. It was common knowledge that she had been and was then the greatest whore there ever was in Rome.' She was never that, but this opinion showed the depths to which the Borgia reputation had fallen.

Ever since the death of Juan, Alexander had been busy reshaping his Borgia dynastic scheme. He had been thwarted in his ambition to gain the crown of Naples for his favourite son. Now Cesare became the subject of Alexander's grandiose dreams. His first objective was to gain the sovereignty of Naples by stealth, using Lucrezia to ease the Borgias into the Aragonese royal house. The plan was to marry her to a Neapolitan prince, thus hopefully opening the way for Cesare to wed King Federigo's legitimate daughter Carlotta, and thereby making it possible for a Borgia to inherit the throne.

This proposed link with Naples had first been suggested

by Cesare when he was sent – much to the annoyance of the more senior cardinals – to crown King Federigo in Naples in August 1497. After the highly-theatrical ceremony, Cesare spoke to Federigo about a prospective Aragonese royal spouse for Lucrezia, and the king politely promised to consider it. In fact, Federigo was horrified at the prospect of a relative of his being joined in marriage to Lucrezia, a woman 'commonly reputed to have slept with her brothers', as his court councillors informed him. The match between Cesare and Carlotta had also been hinted at, and this obvious first step towards a takeover of his kingdom alarmed the king even more. Because Cesare was a cardinal and therefore not allowed to marry, Federigo felt a certain margin of safety. But how long that comforting feeling would last was a matter of conjecture. He knew the devious ways of the Borgias. He was also horrified by Cesare's lifestyle. The pope's son had laid aside his purple robe after the coronation ceremony to satiate himself with some beautiful ladies in Naples, and he lived with his entourage in spectacular style which left the Neapolitan coffers strained and the royal family nervous. The handsome, athletic Cesare attracted the attention of every woman in the Neapolitan court, and he fell in love with Maria Diaz Garlon, daughter of an Aragonese count. He returned to Rome with a burning ambition to snatch the sovereignty of Naples, and with a sinister souvenir – syphilis. The disease soon passed through its first stage and appeared to subside. Cesare believed himself cured, but the disease, which was only just becoming known to European medical science, was to blight the rest of his life.

In the months following Federigo's coronation while Lucrezia's divorce was being engineered, Alexander took over the negotiations aimed at securing a husband of suitably noble pedigree for his daughter. One by one various suitors were considered. Francesco Orsini, the Duke of Gravina, was an early candidate. The resultant link with the Orsini would offer the possibility of ending the family feud, but Francesco was rejected by Alexander as being too lowly for his ambitions. Ottavino Sforza, another member of the

Milanese family, was undeterred by Giovanni's fate and registered his interest, also without success. For Alexander's eyes and intent were firmly fixed on Naples, which made King Federigo feel extremely uneasy. Alexander asked the king about the prospects of Roberto di San Severino, heir to the Prince of Salerno, but he was quickly put out of the running when suspected links with France came to light. Then Federigo proferred a candidate whose sacrifice to the voracious Borgia appetite he hoped would satisfy them. He sequestered the principality of Salerno and presented it with the title of Duke of Bisceglie, to Alfonso of Aragon, illegitimate son of the deceased King Alfonso and brother of Jofre Borgia's wife, Princess Sancia.

Alexander was still considering the newly-created duke when he was obliged to quell a scandal which was developing around Lucrezia. A rumour had spread that his daughter was incarcerated at the San Sisto Convent to hide from a series of horrendous allegations. While the papal commission was in the process of establishing Lucrezia as a *virga intacta*, so the stories went, she was engaging in incest and other sexual affairs with members of the Vatican establishment. She was reputed to have been conducting a clandestine affair with Perotto Calderon, a young and handsome Spanish chamberlain whom Alexander had entrusted with the delicate task of running messages between the Vatican and San Sisto. It was alleged that in the days when her divorce was being finalized, Lucrezia had become pregnant by Perotto.

This was a scandal of the worst possible kind. Any evidence produced to support it was likely to sabotage his plans for Lucrezia's marriage. The most potent witness would have been Perotto, but his story was never to be heard. Early in February 1498, his body was fished out of the Tiber, 'where it fell against his will', as Johannes Burchard recorded in his diary with grim humour. Was this another contract killing like Juan Borgia's? Within days, Paolo Capello, the Venetian envoy in Rome, was writing of the young chamberlain's fate: 'With his own hand, and under

121

the mantle of the pope. Cesare murdered Master Perotto so that his blood spattered in the face of the pope, of whom Master Perotto was a favourite.' Perotto's death did not end the gossip, for by the middle of March a Ferrarese diplomat was asserting, 'It has been vouchsafed from Rome that the daughter of the pope gave birth to a child.'

If Lucrezia really bore a child then, she would have been pregnant at the very moment she was swearing to her virginity before the papal commission. The truth, as with so many events of the Borgia era, is shrouded in mystery. A child born around this time and christened Giovanni did take his place in the family circle. He became generally known as the 'Infans Romanus' and was invested as the Duke of Nepi in 1501. Two secret Papal Bulls issued in 1502 refer to the paternity, but only further confuse rather than clear up the matter. The first declares that the child was a son of Cesare and 'a marriageable woman'. In the second, Alexander attests to the fact that he himself was the father. A generally accepted conclusion is that the child was the off-spring of Alexander and Giulia Farnese. When Giulia's husband, Orsino Orsini, was killed by a falling roof in a decrepit country castle where he had been kept in virtual exile, the care of Giovanni passed to the Borgias, and Lucrezia in particular. The combined evidence of the child's proximity and the secret Papal Bulls tended to fuel the allegations of incest surrounding the family.

Discontent at what was considered the blatant Borgia immorality and roguery was worsened by the rabid Florentine monk, Gerolamo Savonarola. Alexander had tried to still the flow of accusations by excommunicating the tempestuous Savonarola, but this served only to increase his invective. The monk called Alexander 'a broken dagger', and censured both him and the Curia of the church for their concubines and publicly-acknowledged children. From the pulpit of the Duomo in Florence he thundered, 'Come hither, O degenerate church. I gave you fine raiment, saith the Lord, and you have made it into an idol. Your vessels you turn to pride, and your sacraments to simony. In lasciviousness you have become a shameless whore. You are worse than the beasts, you are a monster and an abomination. Time was when you felt shame for your sins, but no longer. You have built a house of public ill-fame, a common brothel.' In another tirade he screamed, 'They sell benefices, they sell the sacraments, they sell nuptial masses, they sell everything. And then they are frightened of excommunication! When evening comes, one will betake himself to the gambling table, another to his concubine. This poison has reached such heights in Rome that France, Germany, the whole world are sickened by it. Things have come to such a pass that we must counsel all men to keep clear of Rome, and say, "Do you want to ruin your son? Then make a priest of him." '

When rumours of Lucrezia's pregnancy were coupled with lurid tales of incest, Savonarola cried out, 'The time is drawing near when we will turn the stopcocks and open the jakes, and then such stinking filth and fetid matter will issue from the city of Rome as will spread throughout the length and breadth of Christendom.'

His personal campaign against the Borgias reached new and dangerous heights when he called on the sovereigns of Europe to call a council to depose Alexander. He wrote, 'I assure you that this Alexander is no pope, nor can he be considered as such. Leaving aside the fact that he purchases his pontifical throne with simony, and that he daily assigns ecclesiastical benefices to those who pay highest for them; and leaving aside his other vices, well known to all men, I assert that he is no Christian, and does not believe in God's existence.'

Savonarola gave the impression of being a madman, foaming at the mouth as he railed against Alexander's iniquity. His fanaticism worked against his credibility, though he was indeed speaking the truth (Alexander had taken to creating and auctioning Vatican jobs on a grand scale to raise extra money for his family). When the monk began urging people to disobey papal authority, Alexander decided he was a threat. A church court was convened to try Savonarola for heresy. He was found guilty and garrotted on May 23, 1498.

Then his body was burned in Florence's Piazza della Signoria, a warning to all who challenged Borgia authority.

All this had no apparent effect on the course of the negotiations for Lucrezia's marriage to Alfonso of Bisceglie. The handsome seventeen-year-old duke rode from Naples to Rome in July 1498, leaving the main part of his entourage at Marino, a few miles distant from the city, because Alexander wanted his arrival to be a secret. As usual, the Roman people picked up news of his presence, and a chronicler declared him to be 'the handsomest young man ever seen in the Imperial City'. Alexander escorted Alfonso to Santa Maria in Portico for his first meeting with the slender, still child-like Lucrezia. She would have been nervous at the prospect of the encounter. But Alfonso was a suave, gentle, handsome young man, and the couple fell in love with each other at first sight.

Lucrezia and Alfonso spent the next six days getting to know each other. Their rapport and overwhelming love for each other was radiantly obvious to all who saw them. Lucrezia knew that the match had been arranged to smoothe the way for Cesare Borgia into the Neapolitan royal house and that her feelings for Alfonso, and his for her, were a matter of pure chance. Nevertheless, she was delighted with her husband-to-be, who was very different from the clumsy, uncouth Giovanni Sforza. Alfonso's happiness matched Lucrezia's, and he shrugged off the grim warning given to him by an anonymous epigrammatist, who wrote:

The other husbands are not dead, Alfonso, they live.
Two are cheated of their hopes, and your punishment awaits you.
It will help you neither to have drawn your name from Parthenope, nor to be of royal stock.
Your rights, too, will be trampled on.

Alexander was overjoyed at his daughter's sudden and totally unexpected happiness. Her dowry was set at forty thousand gold ducats, but the pope had a clause inserted in the marriage contract which stipulated that the couple must live in Rome during his lifetime. After the traumatic periods of separation forced by Lucrezia's first marriage, Alexander had come to realize that he could not bear to be separated for any length of time from his daughter.

Lucrezia was stunningly dressed for her second Vatican wedding – she wore a gown of jewel-studded silk, a girdle of pearls, and a gold coronet. But this occasion was much more subdued. Only family and close friends were gathered to watch as she knelt beneath the raised sword of the Vatican army commander to vow to spend her life with the handsome boy at her side. The nuptial banquet was also a quieter affair, though it was marred by a fist-fight between the retainers of Cesare Borgia and Princess Sancia. Swords were drawn in the mêlée, and calm was restored only when Alexander stepped in. Remembering the complaints about his behaviour at the first wedding feast, Alexander took care to obey the rule which forbad popes from sitting alongside women, and commandeered a table separated from the other diners. He did, however, have Princess Sancia pouring his wine, and two cardinals to carry his food to him. Afterwards, a play was performed, with Cesare incongruously taking the part of a unicorn, a symbol of chastity.

Johannes Burchard records that the marriage was consummated that very night, and Lucrezia and Alfonso settled comfortably into their home at Santa Maria in Portico, where they surrounded themselves with a literary circle of poets, writers and scholars. In early January 1499, a jubilant Lucrezia announced that she was pregnant. However, women of the time were not encouraged to cosset themselves during pregnancy, and the next month found Lucrezia frolicking with her ladies-in-waiting in a vineyard belonging to one of the cardinals. A healthy exuberant girl, Lucrezia challenged her friends to a race. She tripped and fell, and in the resultant turmoil one of the girls fell on top of her. Lucrezia, in great pain, was carried into the house, and she miscarried a few hours later.

Alexander was stunned by the loss of his favourite daughter's child, and an air of gloom descended over the

125

Vatican. A couple of months afterwards, however, Lucrezia found she was expecting another child. She determined to take more care with this pregnancy, and settled down to a quiet life at Santa Maria in Portico. Her expectations of happiness were to prove short-lived, however, as a shifting of family allegiance placed a question mark over the political viability of her marriage.

8

CESARE STEPS INTO JUAN'S SHOES.

Arguments about future policy echoing through their richly-decorated apartments were a feature of Borgia family life. At the centre stood the volatile Cesare. The purple robe of a cardinal had never rested comfortably on his shoulders. In fact, he seldom wore the robe and usually ignored his church duties. He was a man of this world, more interested in hunting animals and seducing women than in the pious life of a churchman. His jealousy of Juan Borgia had been transparently obvious, as he watched his younger brother accumulating the worldly rewards due to the pope's favourite son. The death of Juan changed all this for Cesare. He now pressed Alexander to allow him to resign his cardinalate and grab the lands, titles and wealth which had been withheld from him while he was checked by holy orders.

Alexander was at first bitterly opposed to this, for he believed that if Cesare remained in the Sacred College, he would one day become pope and take over the role of defending family interests from the throne of St Peter. Alexander hoped that the youngest son, Jofre, would become a true Borgia man and follow the path ordained for Juan. However, the nervous and insipid Jofre soon proved a disappointment, and Cesare emerged as the only candidate vigorous enough to become the flag-bearer for Alexander's ambitions.

Alexander searched Italy for a state which would make a dynastic implantation possible. He examined the smaller states up and down the peninsula with his covetous gaze. Naples had emerged as the most likely territory. It was dynastically weak as a result of a series of deaths and abdications, and plagued by rebellious barons, many of them French Angevins whose loyalty was doubtful at best. Jofre and Lucrezia had already been found a place in the Aragonese royal household, even if their grip was only on the illegitimate line. The next target, firmly in the Borgia sights, was King Federigo's legitimate daughter Carlotta.

The proposal that Carlotta should marry Cesare had first been raised when he officiated at Federigo's coronation. Federigo sidestepped the issue, pointing out that Cesare was a cardinal and therefore unable to wed. The king told Alexander, 'If you can produce a son who can marry my daughter, and remain a cardinal, I would then consider it.' This was an impossibility, as he well knew. But then a papal emissary arrived with word that Cesare would soon be resigning as a cardinal, and would therefore be able to marry. Such a resignation was unheard of, but Federigo reasoned that, if it were engineered, and Cesare were married to Carlotta, a complete Borgia takeover of Naples was inevitable. He had heard the stories of Borgia ruthlessness, and believed, probably correctly, that the family would not shrink from murder to usurp his throne once Cesare was in a dynastic position to seize it. Federigo felt outraged and threatened by Borgia avarice. 'They are never satisfied with what they have', he raged. But he was wary of their inherent power, and, wanting to avoid a face-to-face confrontation caused by an outright snub, declared that he could not make the decision for Carlotta. So he switched the onus to his daughter. If she agreed to the match, he said, then he would allow it. But the decision, he emphasized, would be hers.

Messages passed between King Federigo and Carlotta, who was studying in France and living as a guest at the French court. It transpired that Carlotta had fallen in love with a Breton nobleman and was not prepared to abandon him for the honour of marrying a pope's son. Federigo conveyed her decision and his apologies to Cesare and Alexander, underlining his assertion that he had done all he could to persuade his daughter to accept Cesare as her husband. In fact, if Federigo had seen some political benefit to himself in

Pope Calixtus III (Alonso de Borja) and the
Borgia coat-of-arms *(Mansell Collection)*

Pope Alexander VI
(Rodrigo Borgia),
from a fresco in the
Vatican by
Pinturicchio
(Mansell Collection)

Rodrigo Borgia as a
young cardinal,
from a fresco in the
Vatican by
Pinturicchio
(Mansell Collection)

Lucrezia Borgia as St Catherine, from a fresco in the Vatican by Pinturicchio *(Mansell Collection)*

Cesare Borgia, a portrait attributed to
Giorgione *(Mansell Collection)*

Castel Sant'Angelo, the Borgia stronghold in
Rome, by the 17th-century artist Vanvitelli
(Mansell Collection)

the match, he could have forced the issue. As it was, he was content to repel this Borgia advance and place the blame on his daughter. Alexander and Cesare viewed this tactical defeat as only a temporary setback. They felt sure they would find a way to persuade Carlotta to change her mind.

Despite the fact that other cardinals who tried to resign were invariably rebuffed, the plans for Cesare to leave the Sacred College went ahead. His fellow cardinals had been reluctant to agree to Cesare's admission into their ranks, and they were now equally opposed to his resignation. They did not see why the rules should be ignored for him, and they also feared that a precedent for resignation could open the way for similarly unprecedented dismissals. However, the cardinals were in no position to resist Alexander's power, and it soon became clear that the Sacred College would have to give their grudging consent. One cardinal's diary entry read, 'Everything in God's church is going to rack and ruin.'

Cesare, following his father's detailed advice, concocted a drama of conscience to justify his desire to give up the purple robe and offered a cosmetic camouflage for ambitious and political motivation. In a supposedly secret address to the Sacred College, which became public knowledge, Cesare renounced his cardinalate. He declared that the investigation which concluded he was the son of Domenico da Rignano had been wrong, that he was really illegitimate, and therefore automatically disqualified from the priesthood. He emphasized that he had never felt called to the cloth, confessed that his private life dishonoured the high offices he held, and announced his resignation from all his church posts.

Johannes Burchard wrote an account of this address in his diary: 'There was a secret consistory, in which the Cardinal Cesare Borgia declared that from his early years he was always, with all his spirit, inclined to the secular condition, but that the Holy Father had wished absolutely that he should give himself to the ecclesiastical state, and he had not believed he should oppose his will. But since his mind and his desire and his inclination were still for the secular life, he besought His Holiness Our Lord that he should condescend, with special clemency, to give him a dispensation, so that, having put off the robe and ecclesiastical dignity, he might be permitted to return to the secular state and contract matrimony; and that he now prayed the most reverend lord cardinals to willingly give their consent to such a dispensation.'

The cardinals, who effectively had no choice in the matter, recorded their consent. Those who knew they could not bring themselves to go along with the charade had diplomatically absented themselves from Rome. Alexander's Papal Bull giving final legality to Cesare's resignation had already been written out.

None of the cardinals, nor the interested diplomatic observers, harboured any doubts about Cesare's plans. Paolo Capello, the Venetian ambassador to Rome, wrote, 'The pope, with all the cardinals' votes, has given licence that the Cardinal of Valencia, son of the pope, could put off that hat and make himself a soldier and get himself a wife.'

A problem which had been worrying Cesare was how to replace the lost revenues of his church appointments. Alexander investigated the possibilities of salaried titles from Italian states which, with the French threat at an end, were squabbling between themselves. No Italian sovereign, however, was really interested in allowing a Borgia to gain a foothold on his territory.

Now no longer a cardinal, Cesare again approached King Federigo in his quest for Carlotta's hand. The answer was the same as before, and the cause seemed lost. But then Alexander heard via his diplomatic network that the French monarchy might be prepared to help force Federigo's hand, in exchange for a much-needed papal favour.

Charles VIII of France had died suddenly in April 1498, after knocking his head on a lintel while visiting a country chateau. A distant cousin, the Duke of Orleans, succeeded him as Louis XII, and issued a coronation declaration that he was determined to take possession of his twin Italian birthrights. The first was the Orleanist claim to the Duchy of Milan, which, coming to him through his grandmother, the legitimate heiress, was stronger than that of Ludovico Sforza, who was descended from the illegitimate line of the dynasty. Louis's ancestors had not fought over Milan because they considered the duchy not worth the trouble. The second was the more familiar Angevin claim to the throne of Naples. Alexander realized that Louis could give him leverage over Federigo, but how could he encourage the French monarch to operate for the Borgia interest?

Soon after Louis's accession, the answer came. For Charles VIII had married Anne of Brittany to gain control of that semi-independent province, and now Louis wanted to marry his cousin's widow to assert his own authority over the territory. But there was one impediment. Louis already had a wife, Jeanne de Valois, who was crippled. The new king claimed that his marriage had been forced on him against his will by his father, and that Jeanne's deformation had prevented consummation of the union. The Borgias controlled the papal power which could annul Louis's marriage and gain for them his fulsome gratitude.

Negotiations began and eventually a complicated agreement was arrived at: King Louis could have his divorce, and a cardinalate for one of his sycophantic supporters. In return, the king promised to try to persuade Carlotta and her father that it was in their best interests that the princess should marry Cesare. He also pledged to give Cesare a French dukedom, lands to go with the title, and an income of forty thousand gold francs. These dealings were complete by the time Cesare gave up his cardinalate, and within hours of the supposedly secret consistory the new Borgia champion had received the royal patent investing him as Duke of Valentinois and Count of Diois.

Within a few weeks, Cesare left Rome to try, with Louis's backing, to win Princess Carlotta in person at the French court. Both he and Alexander believed she must fall prey to the combination of Cesare's looks and masculine charm, and a flashy display of Borgia wealth. The whole venture had nothing at all to do with personal passion, for Cesare and Carlotta had never met.

A fortune in church gold was squandered on the wedding gifts and personal baggage Cesare took with him. Six French galleys were needed to transport the load from Civitavecchia to Marseilles, and Cesare was accompanied by an entourage of nearly two hundred. The Borgias were determined to impress, regardless of expense.

Cesare was dressed in velvet and damask, and rode a charger whose shoes were made of silver. He led his procession through the towns of France, a country just emerging from its medieval slumber. The ordinary folk were awestruck by the dazzling splendour of his entourage. At Chinon – the castle renowned as the location of Saint Joan of Arc's historic interview with the Dauphin (later Charles VII), when she urged him to save France – King Louis awaited Cesare with his sophisticated retinue of courtiers.

Cesare's spectacular procession was recorded by a royal chronicler for the family history: 'The Duke of Valentinois entered thus on Wednesday, the 18th day of December, 1498. Before him marched the Cardinal of Rouen, M de Ravestain, the Seneschal of Toulouse, M de Clermont, with many lords and gentlemen to the foot of the bridge. He was preceded by twenty-four handsome mules carrying trunks, coffers, and chests, covered with clothes bearing the duke's arms, then again came another twenty-four mules with their trappings halved in red and yellow, the colours of the king, then twelve mules with coverings of yellow striped satin. Then came six mules with trappings of cloth of gold, of which one stripe was of cloth of gold cut, the other smooth, which made seventy in all. And after came sixteen beautiful great chargers, led by grooms, covered in cloth of gold, crimson and yellow. After these came eighteen pages, each one on a fine charger, of whom sixteen were dressed in crimson velvet, the two others in cloth of gold. These, the people said, must be his two favourites.

'Then came six fine mules richly equipped with saddles, bridles and trappings in crimson velvet, accompanied by grooms dressed in the same. Then two mules carrying coffers and all covered in cloth of gold. The people said that those two must be carrying something more exquisite than the others, either beautiful rich jewels for his mistress, and for others, or some Bulls and fine Indulgences from Rome, or some holy relics. Then after came thirty gentlemen clad in cloth of gold and silver, followed by three musicians, two tambours, and one rebec, dressed in cloth of gold according to the style of their country, and their rebecs had strings of gold. They marched between the gentlemen and the Duke of Valentinois playing all the while.

'Then came four with trumpets and clarions of silver, richly dressed, playing their instruments without ceasing. There were also twenty-four lackeys all clad in crimson velvet halved with yellow silk, and they were all around the duke. Beside him rode the Cardinal of Rouen, conversing with him. As to the duke, he was mounted on a great tall horse, very richly harnessed, with a robe of red satin halved with cloth of gold and embroidered with rich gems and large pearls. In his bonnet were two rows of five or six rubies, large as beans, which showed a great light. On the brim of his bonnet he also had a large quantity of jewels. Even his boots were fringed with chains of gold and edged with pearls. He had on a collar and pendant ablaze with diamonds. The horse he rode was weighed down with leaves of gold and covered with fine jewellery and works of the goldsmith's art, with many pearls and precious stones. Even a mule's harness was covered with roses of fine gold to the thickness of a finger.'

Cesare's entry into Chinon had been designed to impress Louis and his court with the power of the Borgias. But the courtiers read into it an ostentatiousness which confirmed all they had heard about the heavy-handed, avaricious Spaniards. And Cesare was very arrogant – he had been surrounded by unbridled power since he was a small boy. However, his inherent charm and personality eventually shone through to repair any damage caused by that first impression. The thirty-six-year-old King Louis, in particular, took a great liking to Cesare, admiring his skill as a hunter and horseman.

The old Borgia antagonist, Giuliano della Rovere, Papal

Legate to the French court and now back in favour in a time of papal accord with France, wrote to Alexander: 'I cannot refrain from informing Your Holiness that the most illustrious Duke Valentinois is so endowed with modesty, prudence, ability and every virtue of mind and body, that he had conquered everybody; he has found so much favour with the king, and all the princes of this court, that everyone holds him in esteem and honour, of which fact I willingly and gladly give testimony.' A more wary appraisal of the situation came from another correspondent who wrote, 'The king carresses him extraordinarily and often takes him on his crupper on horseback, according to his letters. All the same a Spaniard who is with him, a man of wit, writes to a cardinal relation of his, that he is afraid that within a few years it may be like the honours done to Christ on the Day of Olives when later on Thursday they placed him on the cross.'

For, as soon as he arrived at Chinon, Cesare had given Louis the documents appointing the king's favourite minister, Georges d'Amboise, to the Sacred College, and also the papal dispensation terminating the king's marriage to Jeanne de Valois. Louis was most grateful to be rid of his wife, and thanked Cesare for the work he had put in as a cardinal to see that the marriage was annulled. There was also an unspoken acknowledgement of the part Cesare had played in ensuring that the luckless Jeanne was pressured into signing a false declaration that her marriage had never been consummated because of her physical malformation. Jeanne, turning away from the world of kings and priests in which she had been so unhappy, retired to a convent to become the founder of the Order of the Annunciation. The twentieth-century Catholic Church has passed its own verdict on the events by declaring her a saint.

Once his papal concessions had been delivered, Cesare realized he was in a vulnerable position, and wondered if Louis would keep his side of the pact and try to influence Carlotta. But that matter had to wait while the king began making his own nuptial arrangements. Louis took the royal court, and Cesare, to the castle at Nantes, where, on January

6, 1499, he married Anne of Brittany. His special thanks to Cesare for helping to make the wedding possible were conveyed in his investment with the highest order of French chivalry, the Order of St Michael, and by granting him the lordship of Issoudun. A special dispensation also allowed Cesare and his descendants to utilize the French royal *fleurs de lys* in their coat of arms. So proud was Cesare of his Gallic royal connection that he started signing himself 'Cesare Borgia of France, Duke of Valentinois, Count of Diois, and Lord of Issoudon'.

The amity between Cesare and Louis grew stronger, and the king became determined to help his friend win Princess Carlotta. The fact that Princess Carlotta was not attractive mattered nothing to Cesare, for a kingdom was at stake.

The French court judged Cesare 'the handsomest man of his age', but the unsightly brown rash and dry skin associated with secondary syphilis were beginning to show on Cesare's face, defying the valiant efforts of his physician, Gaspare Torella. This obvious diminution of his attractiveness may have influenced Carlotta. In any event, she quickly made it plain to Louis that she had no intention of marrying Cesare. She reminded Louis that, as everyone at court well knew, she had fallen in love with the Breton nobleman Nicholas de Laval, and was determined to become his wife. No amount of persuasion, flattery or advice about the advantages of joining the Borgia clan could move the young girl. Giuliano della Rovere wrote to Alexander that Louis 'seems so perturbed by this feminine perversity that he has declared that nothing else at the moment is so much on his mind.' The true reason for her intransigence was illuminated when della Rovere concluded, 'Either on her own impulse or through the persuasion of others, she has until now refused to marry the duke, unless her father wills it.'

Alexander knew that King Louis coveted Naples himself, and wondered if he was doing all he could to force the issue. The pope sent the Bishop of Melfi to the French court to investigate. The bishop confirmed that Louis 'has not failed to make every effort that this marriage should come about, having shown signs of wishing to exile her from court.' The threat to order Carlotta out of France did nothing to change the position, and Alexander once again contacted her father to see if there were anything he could do to help Cesare. King Federigo replied that he would not agree to the match unless Louis renounced his claim to the throne of Naples. This was conveyed to Louis, whose response was equally inflexible. The Neapolitan throne, he asserted, was his birthright bequeathed to him by his Angevin ancestors, and his claim to it was not negotiable.

Federigo became alarmed that the incessant pressure might break down his daughter's resistance, and sent two emissaries to remind her that she could not marry without his consent. The princess reassured her father that she was holding firm, and that she had never seriously considered Cesare as a prospective husband. The envoys were then granted an interview with King Louis, but started badly when they offered a pledge in the name of Federigo and his realm. Louis snorted that Federigo was impertinent to take an oath on a realm that did not legally belong to him. Angrily he berated them on the subject of Cesare's proposed betrothal to Princess Carlotta. The encounter became even more acrimonious as the emissaries told him 'to a bastard son of the pope, the king not only would not give his legitimate daughter, but not even a bastard child.' The French king then insulted them about the illegitimate children crowding the ranks of the Aragonese dynasty of Naples, and the visitors responded with disparaging remarks about Louis's family. Louis ordered them out of his court, realizing there would be no further chance of friendly discussion with Federigo.

By February 1499, Alexander was gloomily writing to Cesare that if the marriage did not take place, the Borgias would be the laughing-stock of Europe. For, he pointed out, everyone knew they had spent a fortune dispatching Cesare to France in such style, with the sole purpose of winning the Neapolitan princess. Alexander's despair caused Cesare to consider aborting the mission and returning to Rome in disgrace. But he remained, more in hope than expectation, praying that something would happen to make Carlotta change her mind.

Louis noticed Cesare's disillusion, and set up a private dinner with himself, Cesare, Carlotta and Anne, the woman he had married after the Borgia dispensation. A resulting rumour circulated the court, to the effect that the nuptial match had been agreed, but within days della Rovere was writing to Alexander, 'The marriage of Duke Valentinois with the daughter of the king was now totally excluded.'

There had never been any real prospect of the marriage succeeding. Federigo had let his daughter know that he would never allow her to marry a Borgia. Her attachment to Nicholas de Laval was a trick to divert Cesare's attention, for Federigo had even thought up that ruse on his daughter's behalf.

Cesare felt bitter and humiliated at his public rejection by the unattractive Carlotta. He was eager to return to Rome as soon as possible, to nurse his damaged pride in the seclusion of his Vatican rooms. But he still hoped to snatch a Borgia advantage out of his French mission. He spent a lot of time with Louis, discussing their respective plans for the future and the options open to them. It was during these talks that a strategic plan germinated in his mind. He knew the barons of the Romagna were once again openly flouting papal authority and ruling their lands without even cursory reference to the pope. He also realized that the papal armies were not strong enough to bring the feudal lords to heel. The means to help him achieve just this were, however, within the power of his friend, King Louis.

Between them, they negotiated a treaty whereby Louis would supply Cesare with an army of six thousand, consisting of both cavalrymen and infantry, and paid for out of the French exchequer, to subjugate the Romagna. In return, Cesare would accept conscription into Louis's army for an attack on Milan, while Alexander would issue papal approval for a French takeover of Ludovico's dukedom, and backing for Louis's claims in Naples. Alexander, angered by

Federigo's embarrassing intransigence over the marriage, and regarding the friendship of the Sforza regime as extremely suspect, accepted this new deal. He was aware that his volte face put Italy in grave danger of an irresistible French incursion, but of more importance to him was the family interest in the Romagna, and a satisfying blow against the arrogance of Federigo.

The pope did not let his Italian adversaries know what was being planned. For Ludovico Sforza and King Federigo were busy setting up a Milan-Naples alliance as protection against French expansionism, and hoped Alexander would add the weight and authority of the papacy to it. Alexander maintained a pretence of considering their offer until his compact with Louis was finalized. Deliberations at the French court were approaching a firm agreement, with Cesare being assisted in the final stages by Giuliano della Rovere, who, for once, concurred with Borgia stratagem. The first that Ludovico Sforza and King Federigo knew of the papal-French alignment was when they received letters from King Louis proclaiming that he would defend Alexander from any attack mounted by them. To back up his commitment, Louis dispatched one thousand French troops to be garrisoned in Rome at his own expense.

Ludovico felt even more in danger when he heard that Louis had signed an agreement with his neighbours, the Venetians, to carve up Milan between them. A space was left on the document of alliance for the pope's name. When Alexander signed, Ludovico knew he was doomed. His cousin, Cardinal Ascanio Sforza, still the church's Vice-Chancellor, rebuked Alexander for his collusion with France which was placing Italy in jeopardy. Alexander's retort, harping back to the French invasion of a few years before, was, 'Are you aware, Monsignore, that it was your kinsman who invited the French into Italy?'

King Ferdinand of Aragon felt equally threatened by the links Alexander was forging with France. He sent envoys to appeal to Alexander to pull back before it was too late, and backed up the plea with a threat to call a council aimed at dethroning the pope. Alexander felt a certain trepidation about the amount of faith he was placing in the goodwill and honest intentions of Louis, but, trusting Cesare's judgement, he held firm. The Spanish emissaries reproached Alexander for his nepotism, and suggested that Juan Borgia's savage murder had been a divine retribution for Alexander's abuse of his papal powers. They delivered Ferdinand's demand that Cesare be called back from France and reinstated as a member of the Sacred College. His misuse of the trust placed in him by the cardinals responsible for his election, they asserted, made questionable Alexander's right to occupy the papal throne. Alexander was furious, and he verbally castigated the visitors. Queen Isabella's private life was far from being above reproach, he said, and pointed out that the Aragonese rulers had no direct heirs. Was this not a sign of divine punishment?

Alexander's aggressiveness, however, belied the nervousness he felt at making enemies of the powers surrounding him. He recruited a trusted personal guard, and kept them around him whenever he set foot outside the Vatican.

While Cesare's political negotiations with Louis were being tied up, a beautiful sixteen-year-old girl in Anne of Brittany's entourage had caught his eye. She was Charlotte d'Albret, a member of a noble Gascony family, related to the new queen of France through her mother, and sister of King John of Navarre. Though not as valuable a match as Carlotta of Naples, Charlotte had two main advantages: her royal blood and her beauty. The Italian envoys who saw her described her in reports as 'the loveliest daughter of France' and 'unbelievably beautiful'. King Louis wrote to Alexander, commending the match. The pope was not over impressed with the French court's record of arranging marriages, and wrote to inform Louis that in the eyes of the watching world, the matter had caused, 'a diminution of our honour and standing, but also that of Your Majesty. May Your Sublimity consider what targets of ridicule are we ourselves and the duke who, having laid down the honour of the cardinalate and renounced all benefices and revenues, remains excluded from that marriage which the princess, as Your Majesty writes, from her own perversity and induced by perverse counsels, has refused.'

He concluded, 'However, since Cesare has written that that cousin of yours pleases him, willingly we consent to the will and judgement of Your Majesty.'

Charlotte's father, Alain d'Albret, a country squire, extracted all he could from the match. The wedding gifts brought for Carlotta of Naples – the gold and silver tableware, silks, jewels and other precious stones, pearls and gold trinkets – were given to Charlotte instead. Louis paid a royal dowry, thereby relieving Monsieur d'Albret of that obligation, and Charlotte's brother, Aymon, was made a cardinal. Cesare entered into the marriage with a high degree of enthusiasm, for he wholly agreed with a contemporary diarist's assessment of the bride – 'the beauty of the lady was equalled by her virtue and the sweetness of her nature.'

The marriage contract, reflecting the realities of Cesare's life, read like a political treaty. Its rambling introduction noted King Louis's consent to the union, being 'duly of the great and commendable services which the high and powerful prince don Cesare de Borgia, Duke of Valentinois, has rendered to him and to his crown, and hoping that the aforesaid duke, his relatives, friends and allies will render unto him in the future, and likewise for the conquest of his kingdom of Naples and of his duchy of Milan.'

Queen Anne allowed the couple the use of her private chapel at Blois Castle for a simple wedding ceremony on May 12, 1499. The whole of the royal court were guests at a sumptuous wedding breakfast given under silk tents in meadows outside the castle walls. The marriage was consummated that afternoon. Johannes Burchard noted in his diary: 'A courier from France arrived in Rome, who announced to Our Most Holy Lord that his son, the former cardinal, had contracted matrimony with the magnificent lady, and on Sunday the twelfth of this month, had consummated it; which he did eight times in succession.' The accomplishment was confirmed by King Louis, who had supplied similar intimate details of his own wedding night with Anne of Brittany. He wrote to Alexander, confessing that, in all humility, he could not match Cesare, with whom the king seems to have been competing in virility. An Italian envoy recorded, 'Valentinois has broken four lances more than he, two before supper and six at night, since it is the custom there to consummate the marriage by day.'

Cesare also recounted his carnal activities to his father. This was not just a matter of boastfulness – consummation, as his family well knew, was a most serious business and had to be verified in writing as soon as possible.

A more comic aspect of Cesare's wedding night was witnessed by Charlotte's ladies-in-waiting, who peeped in on the couple's embraces. Cesare had ordered aphrodisiac pills, but a practical joker had replaced these with purgatives. This gave the ladies-in-waiting an evening of laughter. The events are recorded in the memoirs of Robert de la Marck, Lord of Fleurange: 'To tell you of the Duke of Valentinois's wedding night, he asked the apothecary for some pills to pleasure his lady, from whom he received a bad turn, for, instead of giving him what he asked for, he gave him laxative pills, to such an effect that he never ceased going to the privy the whole night, as the ladies reported in the morning.'

Charlotte had been attracted to Cesare by his superb physique and wrote a letter to her father-in-law, declaring herself to be well satisfied with her husband. Cesare also wrote to Alexander, describing himself 'the most contented man in the world'.

All the letters from France, with their fulsome details of the wedding night, were read out to a public consistory by Alexander. The pope had been so pleased to hear of the marriage that he ordered celebration bonfires to be lit throughout Rome, including one before the gates of Santa Maria in Portico. Burchard, however, felt that the Borgias had been dishonoured by the snub from Naples, and did not consider the wound healed by the new match. In an unenthusiastic diary entry, he recorded, 'This took place as a sign of rejoicing. In fact, it was a great dishonour, a great shame for His Holiness and the Holy See.'

Cesare and Charlotte spent their two-month honeymoon at a castle on his new ducal estate of Valentinois. Their brief happiness ended when King Louis called on Cesare to command a squadron of heavy cavalry in his invasion of Milan, aimed at claiming the Orleanist birthright to the duchy. Charlotte was pregnant when Cesare left Valentinois, and was to give birth to a daughter the following spring. But Cesare was destined never to see the child, nor to set eyes on his wife again. Meanwhile, he wrote to her often and sent expensive gifts.

The French sweep into Italy was another triumphal procession. One by one the Milanese strongholds surrendered in the face of the French military. With the Venetians pressing in from the east to grab their share of the spoils, Ludovico Sforza realized his position was hopeless. The arrogant duke had been known to boast that the pope was his chaplain, the Venetians his treasurers, the Emperor Maximilian his *condottiere* general, and the king of France his messenger. Those days vanished as he fled ignominiously to the refuge of the Tyrol mountains, while King Louis and Cesare led the victorious French army's entry into his capital city of Milan.

The military parade was watched in glacial silence by the Milanese, though even they had to admire the new ceremonial sword which hung at Cesare's side. Monogrammed 'CESARE', engravings on it depicted the triumph of Cesare, and Caesar's crossing of the Rubicon. Acknowledged as the most beautiful sword in the world, it reflected its owner's personality. For, like his namesake, Cesare was monumentally ambitious.

King Louis took over Ludovico Sforza's residence at the Castello Sforzesco, and discovered that the oaken jewel chests, with impregnable locking devices invented by Leonardo da Vinci, were lying open. Unfortunately for Louis, the duke had taken his legendary and priceless collection of jewels and pearls with him into exile.

The invaders were very impressed by the elegance of Milan. Ludovico Sforza, as a usurper of the throne, had sought to overawe his new subjects by investing a fortune in patronage of Renaissance art, and had employed Leonardo for several years. The Renaissance genius which their partnership bequeathed to the city is perhaps best expressed by the painting of The Last Supper, which still adorns the refectory wall of the Santa Maria delle Grazie monastery. Even Ludovico's stables were decorated with frescoes of his horses.

The sophisticated Milanese viewed their conquerors as barbarians. The French army confirmed this opinion by raping women on the streets, and spitting and defecating on the floors of the superb castle rooms. French archers used Leonardo's clay model of an equestrian statue of Francesco Sforza – the formidable *condottiere* who had seized the Milanese dukedom for his family – for target practice, reducing it to a pile of rubble.

With Milan firmly under control, Louis discharged Cesare from his cavalry command and sent the twenty-four-year-old duke on his way to reassert papal rule over the rebellious lords of the Romagna. The French king gave Cesare the army promised in their deal, consisting of 1,800 knights and 4,000 Gascon and Swiss infantrymen, for his conquistadorial mission.

The first shot of the Romagna campaign was fired by Alexander, who declared that, as the papal tribute money was overdue from the feudal lords of Rimini, Pesaro, Imola, Forli, and Faenza, these domains had to be handed back to the direct jurisdiction of the church. The rulers, who exercised a sub-contracted sovereignty from the pope, naturally refused.

The Romagna, which made up the north-eastern section of the Papal States, sat in the strategic gap between the Apennines and the Adriatic Sea. It was fertile country, with mile after mile of vineyards, orchards, and arable farmland. The peasantry of the city-states which had evolved from the enlightened republics of the Middle Ages were subject to the despotic rule of their church-licensed tyrants.

A graphic portrayal of contemporary life in the area is

contained in Machiavelli's *Discorsi:* 'The Romagna was a nursery of all the worst crimes, the slightest occasion giving rise to wholesale rapine and murder. This resulted from the wickedness of these lords, and not, as they asserted, from the disposition of their subjects. For these princes being poor, yet choosing to live as if they were rich, were forced to resort to cruelties innumerable, and among other shameful devices contrived by them to extort money, they would pass laws prohibiting certain acts, and then be the first to give occasion for breaching them; nor would they chastize offenders until they saw many involved in the same offence; when they fell to punishing, not from any zeal for the laws they had made, but out of greed to realize the penalty.'

This campaign transformed Cesare from a devious papal henchman into a redoubtable and much feared conquistador. He emerged as a natural leader of fighting men, inspiring them with the confidence he exuded.

There had been no need for him to fight in Milan, because the conquest there had been made easy by the headlong flight of Ludovico's army. Consequently, his opening test as a military commander came when he led his army to Imola, the first city he was to claim in his father's name. The city gates were flung open by the terrified citizens at Cesare's shouted order, but the citadel garrison put up a valiant resistance. They were overwhelmed by a massive and ferocious assault, brilliantly directed by Cesare, and forced to surrender.

Cesare had survived his first command, but he was puzzled. For Imola and its twin city of Forli were ruled by the vindictive, ruthless Riario family, and he had expected the defenders to be so happy at the prospect of being liberated that they would welcome him with open arms. The answer lay in the enigmatic Caterina Sforza, Countess of Imola and Forli, who ruled as regent for her young son, Ottaviano Riario. Tall, blonde, statuesque, a lover of fine clothes and jewels, a graceful dancer, charming and practical, she was as violent and vengeful as she was sensuous and beautiful, and she instilled fear in her own people. Caterina had become a daunting adversary. When she was thirteen, her father had been murdered. Her first husband, Gerolamo Riario, was killed by an angry mob who seized him and flung him from a high window of his own palace. She avenged his death in the most savage, bloodthirsty manner, but her second husband, Giacomo Feo, was assassinated before her eyes.

During the tumult in Rome after the death of Pope Sixtus IV, Gerolamo Riario's uncle, she rode into the city to take command of the Castel Sant'Angelo in the name of her husband, who had fled in panic. Reports say that when the citizens of Forli threatened to kill her two Riario children in the midst of a revolt, Caterina stood atop her castle, raised her skirt, and shouted, 'Look! I have the mould to make some more!' In war she was courageous and ruthless – she used to perch a falcon on her wrist, and wear a steel corselet over a satin dress. She rode into battle in full armour, wearing a specially-designed breastplate. A remarkable, legendary character, she was dubbed a virago, and the biographer Clemente Fusero described her as 'the toughest, bravest, most splendid female figure in all history: the fierce heart of a lioness in a magnificent Amazon's body.'

Caterina delayed Cesare's advance on Forli by attempting to kill Alexander. She sent him a particularly lethal letter which had lain in the bandages of a plague victim's corpse. If she had managed to kill the pope in this fashion, it would have been a spectacular coup, for with Alexander gone, Cesare's power would have been shattered, and his resultant and essential military support from France would have disappeared. Cesare left his invasion force to dash to the Vatican, where he found his father safe but berating Caterina Sforza as 'the daughter of iniquity'. Mercilessly Alexander ordered that the two bearers of the letter, which had been delivered in a sealed container, should be burned at the stake.

Caterina faced Cesare as he led his force to the city of Forli. Lesser strongholds had surrendered without a fight when they heard of the fall of Imola, and the citizens of Forli displayed no wish for a battle. They capitulated to Cesare –

'like whores!' fumed Caterina – after a brief resistance. The French infantry rewarded them by sacking the town and massacring indiscriminately. Caterina, who had retreated to the comparative safety of her nearby fortress of Ravaldino, was delighted, declaring that her people had received a well-deserved punishment for failing her. She then ordered that hostages from Imola, held to guarantee against the surrender which had, nevertheless, taken place, should be beheaded.

When Cesare's army ranged itself before the Ravaldino fortress, he called on Caterina to surrender her garrison of two-thousand. Predictably she refused, but suggested a parley with Cesare on the drawbridge. Cesare suspected a trap, and only just managed to avoid being scooped inside when the bridge was suddenly hauled up. A furious bombardment was directed at the stronghold for two weeks until the wall was finally breached.

Cesare wanted to deal with the amazing Caterina personally, and offered a reward of ten thousand ducats to whoever captured her. His artillery breached the wall of the fortress, and the infantry charged through the gap in a furious assault. Caterina fought alongside her men with sword flailing, dealing lethal blows all around and howling like a wild beast. Four hundred men died in thirty minutes of carnage, but the defenders resisted heroically until Caterina herself was captured. By then corpses were scattered in the ditches, on the battlements, and around the courtyard. A witness described the scene after the battle had subsided as 'like a glimpse through the gates of hell'.

The battle for Ravaldino over, Cesare's Swiss mercenaries turned their attention to looting the town of Forli. They were thus engaged when Cesare, seeking the loyalty of the citizens, ordered his troops out of the town. This may have gained him the thanks of the townfolk, but the Swiss were less grateful. For when Cesare called on them to prepare to march on Pesaro, the city ruled by Lucrezia's ex-husband, Giovanni Sforza, the men's leaders announced they would not fight unless their pay was increased to compensate them for their losses caused by the ban on looting. Cesare had the mutineers drawn up, supposedly for a review parade. Then he ordered the siege artillery to be trained on the lines of soldiers while he rode up and down chastizing them and threatening to blow them to pieces.

The revolt collapsed, but Cesare's conquering army was never to reach Pesaro. As they prepared to leave Forli, news came from Milan that Ludovico Sforza, backed by an army of Swiss and German mercenaries, had re-entered his capital. Cesare's French troops were consequently ordered back to Milan. Without them, Cesare realized that further conquests in the Romagna would not be possible. So he took the oaths of fidelity from the citizens of Imola and Forli in his father's name, reinstated Caterina's officials, and left garrisons to hold the strongholds he had taken. Then he headed south, taking Caterina Sforza with him. One account claims he was violent with her, and ordered that his tempestuous prisoner should be whipped. Another chronicler declared, 'He is taking his pleasure,' and the general consensus seemed to be that Caterina was attracted by her handsome captor and that they had an affair as Cesare made his way to Rome.

The triumphal entry into Rome on February 16, 1500, was yet another grand Borgia procession. The cardinals and ambassadors to the Holy See joined Jofre Borgia and Alfonso of Bisceglie to greet Cesare, the returning hero, at the Porta del Popolo. The city was crammed with Holy Year pilgrims, thousands of whom turned out to watch as Cesare, dressed in a full-length coat of black velvet and wearing his gold collar of the Order of St Michael, led the way, followed immediately by his personal guard, who had his name spelt out in silver letters on their jackets. His troops rode or marched behind, surrounding the captive Caterina Sforza. She was also dressed in black from head to foot and was manacled with fetters of gold. The dramatic effect was heightened when trumpets heralded the procession's approach to the Castel Sant'Angelo, and the cannons of the fortress thundered a salute to the victorious Cesare.

Johannes Burchard recorded, 'Some two hundred or more

explosions in turn shook the area, coming first from the tower in the castle garden, then from the round tower facing the bridge with reverberations that brought down some windows and shutters, then from the tower facing Santo Spirito, next along the whole length of battlements, and finally from the highest tower in the castle.' Alexander awaited his son at the Vatican, and was so pleased to see him that he laughed and cried at the same time. Cesare, attempting to adhere to expected formalities, made as if to kiss the papal foot, but Alexander stepped forward to hug him.

The parade, observers noted, had been a spectacle of which Cesare's Roman predecessor, Julius Caesar, would have been proud. The connection was emphasized when the very next day a pageant containing eleven floats with displays based on Caesar's exploits was mounted in the Piazza Navona.

Upon Cesare lay all the Borgia hopes for the future which had previously been invested in Juan, and within weeks he stepped firmly into his dead brother's shoes when Alexander appointed him Captain-General of the Church. He was also awarded the Golden Rose, the highest military honour the church could bestow. Alexander told him during the ceremony in St Peter's: 'For all faithful Christians, this flower, the most beautiful of all, symbolizes the joy and the crown of the saints. Receive it, very dear son, you who add great virtue to nobility.' Those who suspected that Cesare had murdered Juan to usurp his position at the papal court nodded knowingly.

This promotion was a natural one for Cesare, confirming his role as leader of the church's soldiers of Christ. Even when a cardinal, he had spent much of his time training with weapons instead of attending to church duties, and the brief but successful Romagna campaign had identified him as a warlord of formidable abilities. Cesare marked the appointment by adding the pontifical keys to the Borgia bull and the lilies of France on his personal coat-of-arms.

Any further military adventures, however, would have to await the French reconquest of Milan. The enforced inactivity was a devastating blow to Cesare's ebullient spirit. He was hungry for glory, and wanted it quickly, for an astrologer had warned him that his time on earth was limited. He confided to friends, 'I know that at the age of twenty-six I am in danger of ending my life in arms and by arms, and since this is so, I must live to enjoy the time.'

Cesare tried to find a substitute for military activity in a hectic social round. He organized a bullfight in the Piazza San Pietro, and astounded the crowd with his performance. Six bulls were let loose, and Cesare, armed with a lance, tackled them on horseback. He killed five of them before he dismounted, picking up a double-handed sword, and cut off the last bull's head with a single blow. Hunting expeditions in the countryside filled his days and when he remained in Rome – now being rebuilt into a magnificent city of spires – he pursued the ladies. Much of his attention was taken up by Fiammetta de' Michelis, a beautiful, educated, wealthy courtesan who became his mistress. Meanwhile, his absent wife, Charlotte d'Albret, wrote to announce that she had given birth to a daughter, Luisa.

9

A MURDER IN THE VATICAN

Cesare's French alliance meant trouble for anybody with Milanese or Neapolitan allegiances. Alfonso of Bisceglie was well aware of this, as was Cardinal Ascanio Sforza, who invented a hunting trip to leave Rome in July 1499, and did not stop until he reached Milan. When Alexander heard of his Vice-Chancellor's flight, he ordered him to return immediately or risk the loss of all his positions and salaries, but the cardinal ignored this letter.

Days later, Duke Alfonso left the city, exchanging the uncertainty of Rome for the sactuary of a Colonna fortress at Gennazano. Alexander was even more furious about this desertion than the sudden exit of Cardinal Sforza, for he read family disloyalty in it. The pope dispatched a company of troopers to ride out to Gennazano and reclaim his son-in-law. They were too late to catch Alfonso, but they did intercept a messenger carrying a letter from him addressed to Lucrezia. In it, the young duke asked his wife to escape from the Vatican and join him. Alexander was angered by this apparent attempt to separate him from his daughter again, and he made Lucrezia write to Alfonso, asking him to come back to Rome. Lucrezia, who was over six months into her second pregnancy, was very sad at the prospect of being separated from her much-loved husband. She did not know that Alfonso had written to her, for Alexander destroyed the letter, but she correctly blamed her father and his political manoeuvring for placing her married life in jeopardy. Alexander vented his anger on Alfonso's sister, and ordered the reluctant Sancia back to Naples. He snorted that if King Federigo did not want to leave Alfonso in Rome, he did not want anything belonging to the king in the Vatican.

Lucrezia's unhappiness and recriminations finally weakened Alexander, and he directed that his daughter should be sent to the papal city of Spoleto as governor. Her brother Jofre, who had been incarcerated in the Castel Sant'Angelo after an altercation with the city police, was released to accompany her. The journey to the ancient walled city, seventy miles distant, and set on a hilltop rising out of the Umbrian plain, took a laborious six days. It was long and hazardous for a woman in the later stages of pregnancy to undertake on horseback, and the pace was deliberately leisurely because of fears that she might miscarry again. With her entourage of noblemen and ladies-in-waiting, not to mention forty-three carts groaning under the weight of clothes and supplies, she entered Spoleto escorted by four hundred infantrymen. The fascinated townspeople turned out to stare at this already-legendary nineteen-year-old daughter of the pope as her procession made its way through specially-constructed papier mâché triumphal arches to the carnival-like accompaniment of fireworks and music.

Lucrezia proved a capable city governor, administering justice in a decisive and impartial manner. She set up a complaints court similar to Alexander's in Rome, and won many admirers for her acute mind and gracious manner. It seems certain that her father wanted to groom Lucrezia as a ruler of at least some of the lands he planned to grab on behalf of the Borgias.

Alexander realized how much Lucrezia missed her husband, and struggled to persuade Alfonso that no dangers lurked for him in Rome. He sent an emissary to Federigo in Naples, assuring him of this, and the king responded by pressuring Alfonso. By late September, some six weeks after he had left, the duke was riding into Spoleto to be reunited with Lucrezia. They spent four days together before setting out for Nepi, an Etruscan papal town on the road to Rome, where they met up with Alexander. The pope was at pains to assure Alfonso that the French alliance need not affect their friendship in any way. Alfonso said he accepted this, but secretly held grave reservations. For he feared that a mis-reading of Borgia intentions could be very dangerous for him.

The couple returned with Alexander to Rome where, on October 14, Lucrezia gave birth to a son. The pope was so excited at the event that he had all the cardinals and ambassadors in the city hauled from their beds before dawn to make the announcement to them. He thanked Alfonso by giving him a command in the papal army. The baby, dressed in a baptismal robe of gold brocade, was named Rodrigo after his grandfather, who officiated at the ceremony in the Sistine Chapel. Shield-bearers, chamberlains, and musicians took part in the celebration, which was witnessed by the cardinals and ambassadors. Young Rodrigo was given a gold bowl and jug, and tapestries were hung in the chapel. It was another flamboyant Borgia occasion, and raised the now familiar howl of disapproval. The Venetian diarist, Girolamo Priuli, wrote, 'There was much murmuring through all Christendom and it was said that the pontiff, the head of the Christian religion, was making a public demonstration of his love and affection for his family, and that the pope was officially declaring himself the father of his children.'

This apparent family amity and exultant happiness for Lucrezia was taking place in a Vatican from which Cesare Borgia was noticeably absent. He had been in France arranging his own marriage, and was at that time fighting his way through Milan and the Romagna. When he arrived back in Rome, he appeared friendly towards Alfonso, who rode with him in the triumphal procession. But the ambitious Cesare feared that his brother-in-law might persuade the pope to choose pan-Italian loyalty to the Kingdom of Naples in preference to a continuing French alliance. He knew that such a reversal would end his dreams of conquest in the Romagna, which he was already seeing as the cornerstone of a state under his own sovereignty. So Cesare coldly decided that Alfonso would have to be dispensed with, even at the expense of his sister's happiness.

Cesare patiently waited for months, until July 15, 1500,

when Duke Alfonso dined with Alexander, Lucrezia, and Sancia (who had been allowed to return to Rome) at the Vatican. Lucrezia and Sancia stayed behind to nurse the pope, who was suffering from one of his periodic bouts of ill-health, while Alfonso prepared to walk the short distance back across the Piazza San Pietro to his home in the palace of Santa Maria in Portico. He left the Vatican by a side door and was halfway across the square when five men he had taken to be Holy Year pilgrims asleep on the steps of St Peter's responded to a shouted signal and rose to rush him, brandishing swords. So surprised that he was unable to defend himself, Alfonso fell under a flurry of blows and sword thrusts. His skull was split open, and he was stabbed in the shoulder, legs and arms. His assailants tried to drag him in the direction of a group of mounted accomplices waiting nearby, but he was rescued by his gentleman-in-waiting and his master-of-the horse, who had both been walking some yards behind, and the two men hauled the duke back to the main Vatican gates. They hammered frantically on the doors to raise the guard, who finally arrived to carry Alfonso up to the Borgia rooms. Lucrezia fainted when she saw her husband with his clothes in shreds and covered in blood. Alfonso regained consciousness, propped up in bed with Alexander, Lucrezia, and Sancia seated around him, at the very moment he was being given the last rites by a cardinal called by the pope.

The attack mystified Alexander at first, and he ordered a round-the-clock guard outside the ornate, frescoed Hall of the Sibyls, which was conscripted into use as Alfonso's sick room. Cesare, as the church's military commander, stepped in to issue an edict that anyone found carrying arms between the Castel Sant'Angelo and the Vatican faced execution. Even these stringent precautions were not enough to make Lucrezia and Sancia feel secure. They barricaded themselves in with Alfonso and, taking turns to sleep, kept a bedside vigil day and night for over a month. They insisted on preparing Alfonso's meals themselves because they feared food brought in from outside the room might be poisoned. And every time the pope's physician arrived to tend Alfonso, they watched the doctor like hawks.

Within weeks, Alfonso seemed to be responding to the care lavished on him by his sister and his wife, and to be well on the way to recovery. But Lucrezia feared that another attempt might be made on his life. She had come to suspect her family's involvement in the incident, and wrote to her father-in-law, King Federigo, begging that he somehow find a way to smuggle Alfonso out of Rome as soon as he was strong enough to be moved.

Cesare was already being regarded as the man responsible for the attack on Alfonso. The day after the assault Vincenzo Calmeta, a papal secretary, wrote in a letter to the Duchess of Urbino, 'Who may have ordered this thing to be done, everyone thinks to be Duke Valentinois.' Paolo Cappello, the Venetian envoy, pointed out the fact that the official investigation was of a most cursory nature when he wrote, 'Who may have wounded him, no one says, and there are no signs of diligent inquiries being made as there should be.' Cesare was allowed to visit Alfonso, but was closely monitored by Lucrezia and Sancia. Later he was heard to remark, 'What is not done at lunch can be done at dinner', which was taken as a clear threat to make another assassination attempt. He also told a friend, 'I did not wound the duke, but, if I had, it would have been no more than he deserved.'

Alfonso was destined never to leave his sick room, but to die there, strangled under the frescoes of the Old Testament prophets. Johannes Burchard gave a cryptic account of the murder: 'He was gravely wounded in his head, right arm, and leg. As he refused to die of his wounds, he was strangled in his bed about eleven o'clock on August 18.' Immediately after the attack, Alfonso's former tutor, the Florentine humanist Raphael Brandolinus Lippus, wrote in a letter, 'Whose was the hand behind the assassins is still unknown. I will not, however, repeat which names are being voiced because it is grave and perilous to entrust it to a letter.'

Lippus recovered his courage some time after Alfonso's death, when he recorded, 'On the advice of doctors, the wounds were already bandaged, the sick man was without fever, or very little, and was joking in his bedroom with his wife and sister, when there burst into the chamber Miguel di Corella, known as Michelotto, most sinister minister of Cesare Valentinois. He seized by force Alfonso's uncle and the royal envoy of Naples, and having bound their hands behind the door, to lead them to prison. Lucrezia, Alfonso's wife, and Sancia, his sister, stupified by the suddenness and violence of the act, shrieked at Michelotto, demanding how he dared commit such an offence before their very eyes and in the presence of Alfonso. He excused himself as persuasively as he could, declaring that he was obeying the will of others, that he had to live by the orders of another, but that they, if they wished, might go to the pope, and it would be easy to obtain the release of the arrested men.

'Carried away with anger and pity, the two women went to the pope, and insisted that he give them the prisoners. Meanwhile, Michelotto, most wretched of criminals, and most criminal of wretches, suffocated Alfonso, who was indignantly reproving him for his offence. The women, returning from the pope, found armed men at the door of the chamber, who prevented them from entering and announced that Alfonso was dead. Michelotto, the author of the crime, had invented the fiction which was neither true nor half true, that Alfonso, distraught by the greatness of his peril, having seen men linked with him by kinship and goodwill torn from his side, fell unconscious to the floor and that from the wound in his head much blood flowed and thus he died. The women, terrified by this most cruel deed, oppressed by fear, beside themselves with grief, filled the place with their shrieking, lamenting and wailing, one calling on her husband, the other on her brother, and their tears were without end.'

This portrayal of Cesare as the cold-blooded architect of his brother-in-law's death who had employed the sinister Michelotto, a professional killer, to choke the life from Alfonso, is confirmed by many other accounts. Paolo Cappello recorded, 'Finally one day Cesare entered the chamber, drove out the terrified women, and called an assassin who strangled Alfonso in his bed.'

The murder shocked Rome, and a cloak of silence fell over the Vatican. Alfonso's body was hastily buried in St Peter's close to the tomb of Pope Calixtus, and no one would officially discuss the death of the nineteen-year-old duke. The Neapolitan ambassador prudently went into hiding. Lucrezia, prostrate with grief, was confined to the Borgia apartments, while Alexander and Cesare strove to concoct a story to cover their tracks. For, though the original assassination plot had been Cesare's, Alexander then became implicated. Burchard tells of their first attempts to lay the blame elsewhere: 'The doctors of the defunct and a hunchback who had cared for him were taken to the Castel Sant' Angelo for questioning. The arrested men were freed because they were innocent. As well noted, those who had sent them there knew who the guilty were.' Alfonso's Neapolitan servants were tortured in an attempt to extract fake confessions to the murder. When this failed, the fatuous tale of Alfonso falling from bed and cutting his head so badly that he died was circulated. This obviously proved unsatisfactory, for Alexander and Cesare then started to claim that Alfonso had risen from his sickbed to fire a crossbow at Cesare as he walked in the Vatican gardens. The duke's death, the story implied, had been retribution for this attempted assassination.

The carefully contrived lies did little to hide Cesare's guilt. Cesare had seen Alfonso as a dangerous threat to his plans, and hired a team of cut-throats to hack his brother-in-law to death and dispose of the body. When this plot failed, Cesare managed to convince Alexander that Alfonso was involved in a plot against the Borgia interests. The pope then became an active accomplice to the murder in the Vatican.

This murder established Cesare's reputation for ruthlessness and vengeance, and his contemporaries feared him more than ever. The stigma was to stay with him throughout his life, and be recorded in history. After Alfonso's death, the murder of anyone of note was laid firmly at his door wherever Cesare might have been at the time.

For Lucrezia, the murder marked the end of two years of happiness. She went into deep mourning, insisted on wearing a black veil twenty-four hours a day, and her grief was matched only by her anger at her father for not preventing Alfonso's death. At the same time, she was overwhelmed by a sense of guilt, for she knew that if Alfonso had not married her, he would never have been murdered.

10

ALEXANDER AND CESARE, THE UNIQUE PARTNERSHIP

Waiting in Rome for the signal that he could resume his subjugation of the Romagna was driving Cesare to distraction, especially when a violent summer storm reminded him that the time available to accomplish his plans might be much shorter than he had imagined. A clap of thunder knocked down a Vatican chimney, which in turn collapsed part of the roof of a papal chamber, where Alexander was conducting an audience. The pope was buried in a pile of masonry, and when his body was hauled out, he was believed to be dead. But a roof beam had saved him, protecting him from the worst impact of the collapse. Within a few days, the indefatigable Alexander was conducting his business normally again.

However, this brush with death had highlighted for Cesare his tenuous hold on power. For that power to survive his father he knew his grip on the Romagna must be solid and unalterable. He discussed this with Alexander, and father and son laid the foundations for a unique partnership which would unite the spiritual power of the pope to the aggressive and temporal might of his army commander. Their secret aim was to usurp the power of all the feudal barons of the Romagna while pretending that the city-states were being reclaimed in the name of the papacy. However, once the Borgia domination of the region was complete, this mask of lawfulness would be cast aside, and the expropriated lands would be passed to the hereditary sovereignty of Cesare.

When this was completed, the Borgia team could turn its attention to neighbouring states weak enough to fall into Cesare's hands, and he would expand his newly-created sovereign state as the opportunities presented themselves. The old Borgia dream of an Italian state had been revived, and this time Alexander's ambitions were unbounded. He had consulted an astrologer, the pope told his son, and the seer had predicted that Cesare would be crowned king of Italy.

Only days after Alfonso of Bisceglie had been so savagely murdered in his Vatican sickbed, Cesare, his identity concealed by a mask, rode out of Rome to meet a special emissary from King Louis of France at a country inn. Ludovico Sforza's army had been defeated and the duke himself captured while trying to escape disguised as a Swiss soldier. He had been taken to Lyons, where he was destined to die a captive. French domination of Milan was therefore absolute, and the army which Louis had promised to his friend Cesare was once again available to him. In return, Cesare repledged papal support for French designs on Naples, and agreed to serve as a military commander when the Neapolitan campaign was mounted.

Cesare started recruiting an army to add to the central French contingent of cavalry and infantry. His earlier victories in the Romagna had been gained simply enough, and this had served to build up his military reputation. Consequently, the mightiest *condotierri* commanders of Europe flocked to fight with him. Roman nobility such as the Orsini (the family feud forgotten in their mutual French amity) joined him, and even many of the lords of the Romagna. They were unaware that their complicity, fuelled in part by a desire to display loyalty, would eventually seal their own fate, and they naïvely brought their soldiers to serve under Cesare's command. Swiss and German mercenaries were contracted into the army, which was to grow to a strength of almost ten thousand of the finest soldiers of Europe.

This mighty force was funded by gold which Alexander shamelessly appropriated from the church treasury. Collections made for a crusade never seriously contemplated were diverted into Cesare's war chest. Cardinals were banned from making wills, which meant that their estates automatically reverted to the church, and therefore to the Borgias. Cardinalates and other lesser, specially created church posts were sold for cash. Edicts were promulgated against the Jews, enabling their property to be confiscated. The same device was used against many people the Borgias chose to declare as Marrani, or secret Jews, purely because of their wealth.

By the end of September 1500, Cesare's mobilization was complete, and he set off for the Romagna at the head of his formidable army. He stopped briefly to visit his sister Lucrezia, who was in disgrace for her public display of mourning for Alfonso, and had been temporarily exiled to the papal city of Nepi with her son, Rodrigo. This was a cruel move by Alexander, since the city was full of memories for Lucrezia of the happy days she had spent there with her husband. She defiantly remained in mourning, and signed her letters, 'La infelicissima' ('The most unhappy one').

Cesare resumed the campaign where he had been forced to abandon it earlier in the year at Pesaro. Alexander dispatched a papal brief, declaring his former son-in-law, Giovanni Sforza, excommunicated from the church citing alleged dealings with the Turks, and thereby deprived of his lordship of Pesaro. To avoid being captured by the vindictive Cesare, Giovanni exiled himself to Venice. Two weeks later, Cesare rode into the city to take the oath of fealty, as Captain-General of the Church, from Giovanni's nervous officials.

The next city Cesare headed for was Rimini, some miles north along the Adriatic coast. Under normal circumstances, the people of that city could have counted on the support of Venice. However, the Venetians had problems of their own, with a Turkish army hovering dangerously close to their doorstep, and could not help the citizens of Rimini. The noble family of the city, the Malatestas, followed Giovanni to the sanctuary of Venice, while Cesare stepped in to take over their government.

Faenza, Cesare's third objective along the Adriatic coast, was similarly deprived of Venetian support, but its ruling family, the Manfredis, were popular enough with their subjects to feel able to count on the people's support. When Cesare's army arrived at the city walls in mid-November, the Manfredis refused to open the gates. The city was subjected to a ferocious artillery bombardment. An early victory seemed in the wind when a bastion collapsed, but a follow-up infantry assault was repulsed with heavy losses. A long siege amidst harsh winter conditions became inevitable. Cesare left a force surrounding Faenza and moved on to Forli; which had been previously conquered; there he worked on legislation to establish his rule over those parts of the Romagna already under his control. He spent Christmas at Cesena, the city he had earmarked as the future capital of his Romagna state. The leading citizens were invited to be Cesare's guests for a Christmas festival of feasting, games and hunting. Their new lord was an impressive figure, and a city historian recorded, 'He ran as swiftly as a horse, and many times ran races with the youths, to whom he gave a start and passed them nonetheless. With his bare hands he could break a horseshoe and any thick cord.'

All the other cities of the Romagna which had not yet been taken over by Cesare trembled at the prospect. For their guardians, the major Italian states of Venice, Florence and Milan, were in no position to give them any help. Cesare flaunted his contempt for the impotence of the Venetian republic, which was nevertheless still the wealthiest of all the Italian powers because of her navy and colonies.

In February 1501, he agreed to provide an escort through the territory under his control for Dorotea Malatesta Caracciolo, a young Venetian noblewoman who was one of the most beautiful women in Italy, recently married by proxy to a Neapolitan lord serving in the Venetian army, and on her way to join him. Shortly after Dorotea was delivered to her Venetian escort at the border, a group of Cesare's Spanish guard, following his instructions, kidnapped her and took her to him. The Venetians were outraged and they wanted to send an army to rescue Dorotea, but they were frightened of Cesare's French allies. Venice's ruling Council of Ten dispatched their secretary, Aloise Manenti, to Cesare at Imola to demand Dorotea's return. Cesare treated Manenti with studied contempt, keeping the envoy waiting while he slept late, and then only addressing him from a balcony. He feigned outraged innocence at the suggestion that he had anything to do with Dorotea's disappearance.

When news of the escapade reached Alexander in Rome, he stormed, 'If the duke has done this, he has lost his mind.' He wrote to Cesare, ordering him to return Dorotea. There was no point, he believed, in upsetting Venice to gratify Cesare's lust. However, Alexander's instructions and the Venetian protest were ignored, and Cesare kept Dorotea captive for over two years, while the Venetians, to save diplomatic face, had to pretend they believed his protestation of innocence. Meanwhile, Cesare had made a potentially very powerful enemy.

The siege of Faenza ended in April when the starving and battered defenders finally surrendered, but Cesare admired the way they had resisted, and treated them honourably. Even the Manfredi lords of the city agreed to sign up for service in his army, which now traversed the Romagna, storming and capturing any fortresses that dared to stand out against them. The cities of the Romagna proved no match for Cesare's highly trained troops, and his own expertise. Though his battle experience was limited, Cesare was clearly a brilliant military leader. The campaign was an expensive one, but Cesare managed to offset the cost by plundering the gold he found in each city's treasury.

Some people suspected where the Borgia thirst for conquest was leading. The Venetian ambassador, Gian Lucido Cattaneo, wrote of Cesare, 'He prospers so that no one dares forbid him anything. The pope plans to make him great, and king of Italy.'

By early May, Cesare had conquered a large part of the Romagna. The areas stolen with only a thin pretext of legality were linked into a duchy, and Alexander conferred the hereditary title of Duke of Romagna on his son. The investment was sent, along with a second Golden Rose as acknowledgement of Cesare's superior military prowess.

Cesare's conquests in the Romagna took him to the legal limit of papal power in the church states. However, he began to look covetously in the direction of Bologna and the Tuscan cities of Florence and Pisa, which had been debilitated by years of internal strife. He wanted to seize the wealth of Bologna, but realized that King Louis, who had been paid a protection indemnity by Giovanni Bentivoglio, the city's lord, would not tolerate such a move. The city had, however, sent supplies to help Faenza prolong its siege, and Cesare used this to force Bentivoglio to hand over the mighty Castel Bolognese, which dominated the strategic Via Emilia and the route to Tuscany.

Cesare then complained to the Florentine rulers that they had given assistance to his enemies during the Romagna campaign, and demanded free passage through Tuscany for his army. The Florentines started negotiations with Cesare while sounding an alarm bell at the French court, realizing that Cesare was attempting to add their city to his conquests. But the French were far distant, and Cesare's army was already on the move. It had taken Siena, and was threatening Florence by the time the Florentines agreed to pay Cesare a yearly salary of thirty-six thousand gold ducats under a treaty alliance which called for him to supply a garrison of three hundred troops. This *condotta* was, in fact, a discreet way of paying Cesare protection money.

However, it was not the money which persuaded Cesare to withdraw his army from Tuscany. King Louis was unhappy about Cesare's unscheduled incursions into Florentine territory, and had ordered an army destined for Naples to travel by way of Tuscany. Louis was prepared to accept that Cesare could formulate his own policies within the limits of his home territory of the Romagna. Extending his rule to other parts of Italy was a very different matter. The king wanted to keep Cesare's power in check while he still could, and so he directed his army commanders to see that the new Duke of Romagna left Tuscany, and to use force if necessary. Cesare realized he had little choice and ordered his army to withdraw, but plundered as he went, collecting a pile of valuable booty.

King Louis knew that he would face strong Spanish opposition to his plan to reclaim Naples in the Angevin name. Knowing this was largely because Ferdinand of Aragon coveted the kingdom himself, Louis had devised a clever plot. He had met Ferdinand and, in a secret concordat signed at Granada in November, the two kings had agreed to partition Naples between them. Louis reasoned that this would give him much-needed support in the war of conquest, and that later he could force the Spaniards out. Unfortunately, Ferdinand also had similar plans to turn on his ally and claim the whole kingdom for himself.

The French army was moving into Italy when King Louis ordered Cesare to join it as it passed through Rome on the way south. It was Cesare's greed for the Romagna which had induced him to pass up the alluring prospect of the Neapolitan crown, but now he began to question the wisdom of his decision. An envoy whom Cesare confided in crystalized the dilemma: 'He is displeased and uncertain because his affairs are held in the air. If the French win, they will not take him into account. If they lose and others defeat the French, he will be in a bad way.'

Cesare entered Rome secretly and stayed hidden in the Vatican for six days while he and Alexander discussed policy. They decided that papal consent would have to be granted for the division of Naples between France and Spain. A potent motive was the French army which was currently in Rome.

That same army was to secure the freedom of Caterina Sforza who was still Cesare's prisoner. She had first been lodged in a villa at the Vatican, but when she proved obdurate about legitimizing Cesare's conquest of Imola and Forli with her signature, she was moved to a cell in the Castel Sant'Angelo. None of Cesare's threats could induce her to give way, and it seemed she might never leave the Castel. The French infantry commander, Yves d'Algere, an old admirer of Caterina, heard of her defiance, and intervened

164

on the lady's behalf. At his personal request, she was released by Cesare and sent to Florence, where she spent the remaining years of her life in a house bequeathed to her by one of her deceased husbands, Giovanni de' Medici. She never signed away her rights to Imola and Forli, but such a detail made no difference to the Borgias.

Caterina's place in the Castel Sant'Angelo was not vacant for long. Astorre Manfredi, one of the Faenza leaders who had resisted Cesare so resolutely and served him so loyally after the surrender, was incarcerated in the Castel, because Cesare believed that the people of Faenza could one day prove a threat. The Manfredi hostage was Cesare's insurance against such an eventuality.

The Franco-Spanish conquest of Naples proved even easier than Charles VIII's easy victory some years before. The only resistance came at Capua, the fortress city guarding the road to the capital. Capua was overrun after a very brief siege, and Cesare afterwards directed the brutal sacking of the town. By the time the invaders entered the city of Naples, King Federigo had fled to the island of Ischia. In desperation, he had appealed to the Sultan of Turkey to help save his dynasty, but Alexander had used this as an excuse to support the dismemberment of the kingdom, and issued a Papal Bull giving the northern half to France, and the southern half to Aragon. This invasion, which cost Federigo and his family the Neapolitan throne, had come about because of the Borgias's wounded pride after the rebuff they had received over his daughter, Princess Carlotta.

11

THIRD TIME AROUND FOR LUCREZIA

The quest for a new husband for Lucrezia had been going on almost from the moment Alfonso of Bisceglie was murdered by Michelotto. Candidates were apparently undeterred by the fate of her former husband. Cesare recommended Louis de Ligny, a cousin of King Louis of France, but Lucrezia rejected him on the grounds that she did not want to live in France. Among the other suitors was a member of the Orsini family, Francesco, Duke of Gravini, a man of noble bearing and a renowned *condotierre*. Alexander believed that a marital link with the Orsini would end the family feud, but Lucrezia was not eager to marry again, and returned to the Convent of San Sisto.

Alexander could have forced his daughter to marry anyone he chose, but he knew how saddened she had been by the loss of Alfonso, and was prepared to wait for her to accept a suitor. However, he knew he could not delay too long – his lucky escape from death in the storm and recurring fainting attacks served to remind him of his own mortality. By 1501, he was seventy-one years old, and realized that he would have to find a suitable husband for Lucrezia before he died – without the strength of the papacy behind her, she would be a widow of no importance.

Soon a highly suitable candidate emerged: Alfonso, the twenty-four-year-old eldest son of the ruling Duke Ercole of Ferrara. Alfonso d'Este was heir to the throne of the duchy, a small Italian buffer state set between the Romagna and Venice. The Este family was one of the longest reigning and noblest houses of Italy, and despotic, absolute rulers. Duke Ercole was stunned when an envoy from the pope raised the subject of a possible marriage between his son and Lucrezia. The prospect of the opportunistic Borgia family marrying into his illustrious dynasty horrified Ercole, but there was little he could do. At first, he rejected the match outright, hinting that he was reluctant because of the rampant stories of Lucrezia and her lurid, even incestuous, reputation.

When this did not discourage the Borgias, he considered producing a secret fiancée for Alfonso. A thinly-veiled threat from the papal envoy persuaded him to forget this idea, and a second emissary, sent by Cesare, arrived at Ferrara to spell out some unpalatable facts to the duke. Cesare wanted to annexe the duchy's lands to protect the northern flank of his Romagna state. With the army at Cesare's disposal, accomplishing this would have been a relatively simple matter, and the throne would be taken away from the Este family. However, Cesare would be most content, the envoy told a shattered Duke Ercole, for the Este rule to continue, so long as his sister was married to the heir apparent.

Ercole saw he had little alternative, but he nevertheless contacted King Louis, pointing out that his family had always been pro-French, and begging the king to intervene with Cesare. He wrote, 'Because, to speak freely with His Majesty, we shall never consent to give Madonna Lucrezia to Don Alfonso; nor could Alfonso ever be induced to take her.' The situation was hopeless. Louis was so embroiled in his dealings with Cesare and Alexander that he could not consider denying them this ambition. The French king made it plain that he would not try to influence the Borgias, but offered Ercole the gratuitous advice that he should try to make all the profit he could out of the inevitable match.

The distressed Ercole told his son that Lucrezia would have to marry into their family, but Alfonso made his reluctance for becoming her husband very plain. Ercole understood his son's feelings, but pointed out that because he was a widower he would have to wed Lucrezia himself if his son refused. Alfonso grudgingly agreed to the marriage, as long as a good enough dowry could be negotiated.

The young man was not a particularly appealing catch for

a beautiful, if somewhat notorious, woman. As a youngster, he had shown more interest in the study of artillery than books. The Venetian ambassador said, 'He is accounted as having little sense.' This had been confirmed when, on a muggy July day, the teenage Alfonso and a group of friends walked naked through the streets of Ferrara. An ugly man, with a prominent nose and bull-neck, and a contrary nature, he had been married previously to Anna Sforza, of the Milanese family, who had died in childbirth. He was reputed to have spent more time in brothels than with his wife. However, the Borgias were uninterested in his morals and reputation – it was Alfonso's pedigree which made him so appealing.

Duke Ercole's true feelings about the impending marriage are recorded in a letter he wrote to his son-in-law Francesco Gonzaga, the Marchese of Mantua: 'We have informed Your Majesty that we have recently decided – owing to practical reasons – to condescend to an alliance between our house and that of His Holiness.' Prudence spurred the duke to delete the word 'condescend' and substitute it with the less harsh 'consent'.

Alexander, unaware of the sentiments expressed in this letter, had always equated happiness with rank and social standing, and was excited at the concept of his daughter marrying into the august and ancient ruling house of the Este, and of his grandchild one day sitting on the throne of Ferrara. Lucrezia was unhappy but realized that the match was one she could not refuse. The negotiations began in earnest.

Duke Ercole demanded a dowry of two hundred thousand gold ducats, and the reduction of Ferrara's annual tribute to the papacy to a purely nominal sum. This was a prodigious request, and represented five and six times Lucrezia's earlier dowries. Alexander countered with an offer of one hundred thousand gold ducats, which provoked Ercole to point out how trivial that sum was when it would one day elevate the pope's daughter to Duchess of Ferrara.

The bargaining was held in abeyance while Alexander and

Cesare went on an inspection tour of their fortress strongholds north of Rome, ostentatiously carrying out an inventory of some of their possessions. Included amongst these was the mighty Civita Castellana, commanding the Via Flaminia, which they had refitted with vaulted rooms and Borgia bulls. Over the gateway they had inscribed the motto, 'Viva Borgia'. While they were away Lucrezia was entrusted with the executive responsibility for state affairs at the Vatican.

Ercole's envoys arrived in Rome in September 1501, to discuss the details of the proposed marriage settlement. They reflected the duke's wariness of the Borgias, and the protracted negotiations took into account the number of men needed to escort Lucrezia to Ferrara, and how much that escort would cost. Lucrezia was by now well used to the role of bartered bride, and Alexander listed her finer attributes, including her administrative abilities, demonstrated during her governance of Spoleto and her management of papal affairs during his absence.

The Ferrarese diplomats were entertained at nightly parties and dances given in their honour at the palace of Santa Maria in Portico. Reports they sent back about Lucrezia were full of admiration. Part of one read, 'Lucrezia is a most intelligent and lovely, also exceedingly gracious lady. Besides being extremely graceful in every way, she is modest and lovable and decorous. Moreover, she is a devout and God-fearing Christian. She is very beautiful, but her charm of manner is still more striking. In short, her character is such that it is impossible to suspect anything sinister of her.'

More disturbing for Ercole were the accounts of ribald parties which Lucrezia and the other Borgias attended at the Vatican. Johannes Burchard described one in the following terms: 'On Sunday evening, the last day of October 1501, there took place in the apartments of Duke Valentinois in the Apostolic Palace, a supper, participated in by fifty honest prostitutes of those who are called courtesans. After supper they danced with the servants and others who were there, first clothed, then naked. After supper the lighted candelabra which had been on the table were placed on the floor, and chestnuts thrown among them which the prostitutes had to pick up as they crawled between the candles. The pope, the duke, and Lucrezia his sister, were present looking on. At the end they displayed prizes, silk mantles, boots, caps, and other objects, which were promised to whomsoever should have made love to those prostitutes the greatest number of times; the prizes were distributed to the winners according to the arbitration of those present.'

Another story circulating among Rome's diplomatic corps told of twenty-five women being taken into the Vatican each night for parties attended by Alexander, Cesare and the cardinals. One in particular referred to 'the pope, who keeps his permanent little flock there so that the whole palace is being openly converted into a brothel for every kind of depravity.' Francesco Pepi, the Florentine envoy, wrote that though the pope had a cold, 'this did not prevent him on Sunday night, the eve of All Saints' Day, from staying up till twelve o'clock with the Duke of Valentinois, who had brought prostitutes and courtesans into the Vatican; and they passed the night with dancing and laughter.'

The so-called 'Letter to Silvio Savelli' was being passed around at this time. This was a letter allegedly written from the Spanish campa at Taranto in Naples, to a certain Baron Savelli, whose lands had been confiscated by Alexander. Such was Savelli's hatred for the Borgias that he had the scurrilous letter translated into every European language and circulated throughout the royal courts. Specifically accusing the Borgias of murder, robbery and incest, it called Alexander 'this monster' and 'this infamous beast'. It asked, 'Who is not shocked to hear tales of the monstrous lascivity openly exhibited at the Vatican in defiance of God and all human decency? Who is not repelled by the debauchery, the incest, the obscenity of the children of the pope, son and daughter, the flocks of courtesans in the palace of St Peter? There is not a house of ill fame or a brothel that is not more respectable. On the first of November All Saint's Day fifty courtesans were invited to a banquet at this pontifical palace and gave the most repugnant performance there. Rodrigo Borgia is an abyss of vice and a subverter of all justice, human or divine.'

Elsewhere, the letter lambasted Cesare: 'His father favours him because he has his own perversity, his own cruelty. It is difficult to say which of these two is the most execrable. The cardinals see all and keep quiet and flatter and admire the pope. But all fear him and, above all, fear his fratricide son, who from being a cardinal has made himself into an assassin. He lives like the Turks, surrounded by a flock of prostitutes, guarded by armed soldiers. At his order or decree men are killed, wounded, thrown into the Tiber, poisoned, despoiled of all their possessions.'

Alexander dismissed these accounts, but Cesare reacted strongly. One man who had been telling stories of Cesare's heinous behaviour was thrown into jail. To make certain that his feelings were known, Cesare ordered the man's right hand to be amputated and his tongue cut out. The hand and the tongue were hung from the bars of his cell for all to see. When Alexander heard such stories, he always tried to find an excuse for his son. 'The duke is a good-hearted man', he would plead, 'but he cannot tolerate insults.'

A report of a more comforting nature came from a confidential agent sent by Duke Ercole to Spain with the task of checking out the Borgia claim to noble antecedents. This agent informed the Este court that, after conducting exhaustive enquiries, scrutinizing the relevant documents, and interrogating those persons best qualified to judge, he could guarantee that the family was 'of great age and nobility in Spain'. In fact, the investigator had been intercepted by Borgia spies and bribed to present a favourable report.

Negotiations between Ferrara and the Vatican continued with a great deal more haggling, and Duke Ercole's demands escalated. Alexander haughtily accused him of 'behaving like a shopkeeper' over the matter. Ercole reminded the pope that the Emperor Maximilian of the Holy Roman Empire had urged him to abandon the match. Alexander saw through this ploy, and refused to raise the dowry in response to it. Finally Ercole decided he must take what he could. The dowry was fixed at one hundred thousand gold ducats, with the proviso that Alexander gave Lucrezia clothes, jewellery, gold and silver to the value of another seventy-five thousand ducats. As a gesture of goodwill, the pope also awarded a series of minor church benefices to members of the Este family.

The marriage agreement was signed in a Vatican ceremony, and Alexander gladly gave the formal papal consent required for Lucrezia's and Alfonso's heirs to occupy the throne of Ferrara. The couple were married by proxy in Ferrara, for the Este family wanted to make sure the wedding actually took place and that their son did not meet the same fate as Lucrezia's earlier Spanish suitors. When news of this ceremony reached Rome, cannons boomed from the Castel Sant'Angelo. The Castel was illuminated, and bonfires were lit on parapets throughout the city. There were scenes of wild jubilation, and two clowns on stilts walked through the streets shouting, 'Long live the duchess' (anticipating Lucrezia's elevation by some years) and 'Long live Pope Alexander'. Lucrezia was escorted by three hundred horsemen and four bishops to the church of Santa Maria del Popolo, where she prayed to St Mary to protect her marriage.

Duke Ercole then wrote to Lucrezia in the most affectionate terms, welcoming her to the family. He said that whereas he previously loved her on account of her virtues, the pope and her brother Cesare, he now loved her as a daughter. Alfonso, Lucrezia's new husband, also wrote, but his letters were more formal.

Though Lucrezia was already legally married to Alfonso, a second proxy ceremony was arranged at the Vatican. For her third marriage in the holy palace, the twenty-one-year-old Lucrezia wore a gold brocade wedding dress with sleeves reaching to the ground, and her train was carried by fifty maids of honour. Cesare dressed even more extravagantly, lavishing ten thousand gold ducats on outfitting himself and his horse. One observer described him: 'All one could see was gold, pearls, and jewels'. Alexander, for the third time in nine years, conducted his daughter's wedding. As on both previous occasions, Lucrezia declared she was entering into the marriage 'most willingly'. A gold wedding ring from Alfonso was placed on her finger by his brother, Ferrante. Another brother, Ippolito, who had been made a cardinal by Alexander three years before, brought a box containing the Este family jewels, and handed them to Lucrezia.

The Borgia and Este families held a celebration party at the Vatican, and Lucrezia danced with Cesare only yards from the room in which Alfonso of Bisceglie had been strangled. A parade of thirteen floats, each donated by one of Rome's districts, moved in procession from the Piazza Navona to the Piazza San Pietro. Cesare supervised a bullfight, and plays and pageants were performed all over Rome in honour of the wedding. Alexander also had a medal struck with Lucrezia's likeness on it, bearing a legend on the reverse side: 'Chastity, a thing most precious for virtue and beauty'.

As Lucrezia was destined to become Duchess of Ferrara, she was naturally expected to live in the duchy. She had to leave behind two-year-old Rodrigo, her son by Alfonso of Bisceglie, who was to stay in Rome under Borgia care. She could not take the boy with her, because no husband of the time would allow a wife's son from a previous marriage to live under his own roof. She said goodbye to her own mother, Vannozza de' Cattanei, now an elderly and wealthy woman, but the most traumatic leave-taking of all was with Alexander. The pope was old enough for them both to realize they might never see each other again. Father and daughter cried as they embraced each other in the Vatican courtyard. Lucrezia, wearing an ermine-lined cloak over a crimson and gold dress, then mounted a white mule and rode slowly out to join the vast escort which was to accompany her on the long journey to Ferrara.

Altogether, her escort numbered over four hundred people, including armed men, noblemen and ladies-in-waiting. Cesare had paid for a security escort of two hundred cavalry, as well as musicians to provide entertainment along the way.

Alexander had provided a string of carriages to carry Lucrezia's trousseau and wedding gifts. Adriana del Mila was accompanying Lucrezia to Ferrara as her companion. Cesare and Lucrezia's brother-in-law, Cardinal Ippolito d'Este, were to ride with the entourage until it was some distance from the city gates. Alexander shouted after his daughter that she must be happy, and that she could rely on him if there was anything she needed. Then, with tears streaming down his face, he went up to the highest windows of the Borgia apartments to run from one to the other until Lucrezia disappeared from his sight. This was the last he was destined to see of his beloved daughter.

Alexander demanded, and received, regular reports of Lucrezia's progress to Ferrara, dispatched by officials of the papal towns she passed through during the cold weather of January 1502. She was given rapturous receptions all along the route, as people vied with each other to demonstrate their loyalty to the pope. Cesare insisted his sister should travel by way of his conquered Romagna cities, and the greetings Lucrezia received in these places were the most enthusiastic of all.

Alfonso d'Este, instead of waiting for his new bride to reach their scheduled meeting place, rode out to meet Lucrezia at the Castel Bentivoglio, a royal villa near the Ferrarese border. He was eager to meet the lady he was already committed to sharing his life with, and they appeared to take an instant liking to each other. The next day, the couple made a triumphal entry into the ancient walled city of Ferrara, accompanied by crossbowmen in red and white livery and a horde of trumpeters. The ordinary people of the city noted her beauty and charming manner, and stared open-mouthed at the gold and jewels which covered her. Greeted by Duke Ercole and every member of the court, Lucrezia rode alongside her father-in-law in the procession, acknowledging the cheers of the crowd in a practised, regal mannner. Prisoners released from jails to mark the marriage joined the curious who had flocked into the city for the occasion.

Lucrezia's new home was an apartment in the Castello

Estense, the magnificent edifice dominating Ferrara. The royal family and household gathered there that night for the ceremony known as the *serenata,* when they were to surround the nuptial bed and tease the couple in it, but Lucrezia persuaded Alfonso to forgo this ritual. Trumpets blared as she entered the bridal chamber, the doors were closed, and she was alone with her new husband.

Alexander had written to Cardinal Ippolito d'Este saying he wanted to hear that Alfonso was showing Lucrezia the affection she should expect from a husband, and not that he was neglecting her as he had his first wife. After the wedding night Duke Ercole wrote to Alexander, 'Last night our son, the illustrious Don Alfonso, and Lucrezia kept company and we are convinced that both parties are thoroughly satisfied.' Alfonso's sister Isabella seems to have been even better informed. She told her husband, 'From what I have been given to understand, Don Alfonso took her three times.'

Wedding festivities continued for days with banquets, parties and theatrical shows. The Ferrarese court was impressed by Lucrezia and only Isabella d'Este was cool and unfriendly. She saw Lucrezia as competition for herself at court, and considered that her brother had been 'humiliated into a marriage with the bastard daughter of a foreign priest'.

12

'EITHER CAESAR OR NOTHING'

The easy Franco-Spanish conquest of Naples was followed swiftly by predictable disagreement over the spoils. Massive Spanish reinforcements were rushed in, under the command of the redoubtable Gonsalvo di Cordova, and soon the area of French domination had been reduced to a couple of isolated and besieged castles. Alexander abruptly reverted to a pro-Spanish stance. Cesare, though not openly hostile to King Louis, was secretly pleased, because the French monarch had proved the stumbling block to his hopes for Tuscan annexations to the Duchy of Romagna. He even started entertaining the notion that he might be able to enlist Spanish help for a war of conquest against Florence.

Cesare had returned to Rome to begin setting up the government of the Romagna. Church officials who owed their exalted rank to the Borgias were appointed as civil administrators. The military governors were drawn exclusively from his fiercely loyal Spanish soldiery. By now, Cesare was suffering from a most unpleasant and unsightly manifestation of syphilis. Weeping sores appeared on his face, and he began wearing a mask during all his waking hours. Perhaps because he felt less conspicuous in the dark, he turned night into day, going to bed at five in the morning and breakfasting at four in the afternoon. This strange regime continued for the rest of his life, and Cesare never again appeared in public without his mask.

Undeterred by his physical condition, Cesare adopted the motto, 'Either Caesar or nothing', and dreamt of one day being crowned king of Italy. His experiences with Louis of France's troops had demonstrated to Cesare that he would have to raise an army of Italian and Spanish *condotierri*, who would place their loyalty to him above all else. Feudal lords enlisted, bringing with them peasants who they had recruited to the military by paying them more than could be earned in the fields, and promising more riches to be plundered. Cesare assembled an army of nine thousand men, half of whom were under his personal command. His own troops were easily identifiable. Dressed in red and yellow livery, they had the name Cesare emblazoned in huge letters on their breasts and backs.

The cities of the Romagna which had evaded capture by default in the earlier campaign soon fell into Cesare's hands. Most gave up without a fight, and those which resisted were battered into submission. Much of his success was due to the attention he paid to military intelligence, which kept him always one step ahead of his enemies, and he developed a legendary reputation for swiftness of movement and dramatic coups. And, with operations which were designed to lose as few men as possible, he earned the unmitigated loyalty of his ordinary soldiers.

Cesare broke off in mid-campaign to head for Milan, where he wanted to collect a reassurance of French support from King Louis. On the way, he stopped at Ferrara to visit Lucrezia, who was pregnant and had contracted such a serious fever that the pope was demanding daily bulletins on the state of her health. Cesare disguised himself as a knight of the Order of St John of Jerusalem to slip out of his encampment, and he walked thus unannounced into Lucrezia's sickroom. She woke to see what she believed to be another delirious vision hovering over her bed, and her fever instantly worsened. Cesare felt so guilty that he lingered at Ferrara until his sister recovered, and took over the responsibility for the bulletins sent to Rome.

King Louis greeted Cesare affectionately, like a long lost brother, when they met, and the French monarch's obsession with Naples led him to promise Cesare a free hand against even the barons historically friendly to France. In exchange he sought, and received, Cesare's pledge of continuing

Borgia military support in the Neapolitan kingdom.

The Duchy of Urbino, controlling a vital mountain pass into Tuscany, was Cesare's next target. He began the assault surreptitiously by approaching the duke, Guidobaldo da Montefeltre, an old Borgia ally, to ask to borrow some artillery pieces. Guidobaldo readily agreed, and sent fraternal greetings along with the machines of war. He was astonished when he found that Cesare had ranged the weapons to threaten his own fortress headquarters at Urbino. He fled for his life, reaching Mantua, some miles to the north, in a state of exhaustion. Guidobaldo called Cesare's ploy 'the great betrayal'. Cesare, who justified the move by claiming that Guidobaldo was at the centre of an anti-Borgia conspiracy, had overthrown the mighty Montefeltre family without firing a single shot. He later tried to placate Guidobaldo by suggesting he accept a cardinalate in exchange for his hereditary rights, but the duke turned this down.

Concerned about the security of the lands he had conquered, Cesare employed Leonardo da Vinci to inspect his defence systems. Leonardo's sketches of the archers, musketeers, and Swiss foot soldiers of Cesare's army still exist, and he took his task as military architect and engineer very seriously, designing fortifications and producing strategic maps. Cesare's faith in him was shown by the letter Leonardo carried which ordered every garrison commander to give him full information about all fortifications and to follow his instructions for improvement.

A Tuscan compatriot of Leonardo's, Niccolo Machiavelli, arrived in Urbino after the overthrow of Guidobaldo to interview Cesare on behalf of the government of Florence, who were extremely nervous about future Borgia intentions. Machiavelli considered the ploy used against Urbino a masterstroke, and greatly admired Cesare's agile brain. He later used the Borgia duke as the model for his book, *The Prince*, which preached that if an absolute ruler wanted to retain power, he had to be absolutely ruthless. His first impression of Cesare, recorded shortly after Urbino, was that 'This Lord is truly splendid and magnificent, and in war there is no enterprise so great that it does not appear small to him; in the pursuit of glory and lands he never rests nor recognizes fatigue or danger. He arrives in one place before it is known that he has left another; he is popular with his soldiers and he has collected the best men in Italy; these things make him victorious and formidable, particularly when added to perpetual good fortune.'

Cesare informed Machiavelli that the Florentines would have to decide whether they were his friends or his enemies. His words were backed up when a *condotierri* army took the Florentine city of Arezzo. He agreed to withdraw the troops, but insisted on being paid a fee for doing so. Cesare also suggested an alliance with Florence, which would have tied the republic to him, but Machiavelli correctly surmised that the restraining hand of King Louis would persuade him to put that idea aside.

Machiavelli remained the Florentine ears at Cesare's court, and was impressed by how the Borgia war lord established peace in the Romagna and acted like an enlightened ruler. Where possible, he retained the local officials in their jobs, and often reduced the taxes which had been levied on the city-states by their earlier rulers. He started to mould a uniform government for the whole region, and a circuit court was established, with a judge of good reputation appointed to hear complaints. Cesare's rule was such an improvement after the tyrannical despots whose positions he had usurped that it was destined to be remembered for centuries.

The smaller states of Italy viewed Cesare's victorious progress with alarm. Francesco Gonzaga, Marchese of Mantua, voiced their fears when he said, 'As far as we can foretell, we deem it certain that all of us, one after the other, will perish. We are like men led to the gallows.'

Cesare's *condotierri* commanders, lords of their own lands, also began to fear him. There was no guarantee that the mercenary army would not attack their own lands, and the soldiers were notorious for switching sides to higher paymasters. They talked of 'being one by one devoured by the dragon'.

This fear drove five of Cesare's leading *condotierri* generals – Vitellozzo Vitelli, Lord of Citta di Castello, Gian Paolo Baglioni, Lord of Perugia, Oliverotto da Fermo, Lord of Fermo, Paolo Orsini, Lord of Palombara, and Francesco Orsini, Duke of Gravina – to band together in a conspiracy against him. Knowing their combined forces outnumbered the remaining soldiers under Cesare's command, the five planned to halt the Borgia expansion, and also to topple Cesare. A plan of battle was drawn up: the rebels hoped to trap Cesare in a surprise pincer movement. They were so confident that they even started arguing about how Cesare's lands would be divided up between them.

However, two essential elements were missing from the plot. The first was a strong leader, with the courage to face up to Cesare, and the ability to inspire his colleagues. The second was surprise. For, though they believed their plans to be secret, Cesare's intelligence service kept him well informed of the impending revolt. In anticipation of their move he withdrew to the fortress city of Imola and ordered Ramiro de Lorqua, his loyal spanish military governor of the Romagna, to prepare the defences of all the other strongholds. Alexander sent more Vatican gold to pay for the recruitment of Romagna troops and to hire Swiss and Gascon mercenaries in Milan.

The rebel alliance was signed at an Orsini castle near Perugia in the first week of October 1502. Days later the opening blow of the campaign was struck at Urbino, where Guidobaldo da Montefeltre rode back to reclaim his duchy and become host to the anti-Borgia headquarters.

Cesare confided his foreknowledge of the plot to Machiavelli and said, 'Believe me that this thing is to my advantage, and they cannot reveal themselves at an hour when it will damage me less, nor can I, to strengthen my states, wish for a thing that will be more useful to me; because I shall know this time against whom I have to protect myself, and I shall recognize my friends.' He was confident at the prospect of meeting his former commanders in battle, but Machiavelli considered Cesare's position was precarious. A number of cities, including the Republic of San Marino, quickly joined the rebels' side, and troops loyal to the Borgia cause numbered only three thousand. His French allies were many miles away, and it was clear that a swift, bold attack on Imola would have overwhelmed Cesare.

Fortunately for him, the *condotierri* hesitated, missed their opportunity, and finally lost their nerve as Cesare's reinforcements arrived, led by a detachment of French heavy cavalry sent by King Louis. The rebels had not attacked Cesare when he was weak because they feared his reputation for invincibility. Now they feared his strength. Cesare persuaded them individually to rejoin him, and the conspirators, who had risen against him to save their lands, now agreed to peace for the same reason. Machiavelli noted that, although Cesare was outwardly friendly towards the conspirators, he made sinister references to them and was plotting revenge.

The revolt collapsed within weeks, and Cesare sent word to the five rebels, inviting them to a banquet at Senigallia, a small fortified town on the Adriatic coast of his Romagna state. His 'dear brothers', he wrote, had nothing to fear from him. Three of the *condotierri* – Vitellozzo Vitelli, and Paolo and Francesco Orsini – were waiting at the town gate to greet Cesare. A fourth, Oliverotto da Fermo, was prudently waiting some distance off with his troops. The last, Gian Paolo Baglioni, had been warned to expect a trap, and had escaped to the sanctuary of Perugia. Cesare's accomplice, Miguel di Corella, separated Oliverotto from his men with a display of bonhomie and accompanied him to the gate. Only when he heard the four commanders were there did Cesare ride up to embrace his former enemies, and accompany them into Senigallia. The gates were closed, and the rebels found themselves in the main square, surrounded by a thousand Swiss and Gascon infantrymen. Cesare, still superficially friendly, escorted his guests to a house where the banquet was supposed to take place. Once inside, he started up a flight of stairs, and, at a signal from him, a group of his guards siezed the *condotierri*. The prisoners were bound, and thrown into cells. That night, Paolo and Francesco Orsini were garrotted by Miguel di Corella. The other two were held for some weeks, but eventually met the same fate as their confederates.

Cesare had cunningly outwitted four of the most experienced military captains of Italy. He described the events to Machiavelli, who recorded, 'His face lit up with delight, and he bade me rejoice at the happy event, for he said he had defeated his bitterest foes, men who were, indeed, enemies of order and peace throughout Italy.' Machiavelli applauded 'an admirable deed'. King Louis of France hailed it as 'an act worthy of a Roman hero'. Paolo Giovio, though an anti-Borgia historian, described it as 'a most beautiful deception'. Leonardo da Vinci made a sketch of the moment of betrayal, entitled it, 'The brutal madness of war', and shortly afterwards left Cesare's court.

The coup was a frightening blow to the rest of the Romagna. The *condotierri*'s troops, camped, at Cesare's orders, some distance from Senigallia, were dispersed. The cities which had been ruled by the captured and slaughtered generals surrendered themselves to Cesare, who was already justifying his action. He called the dead men 'public pests, part of that swarm of troublesome insects who are ruining Italy', and presented himself as a hero whose aim was to rid his country of tyrants.

Even those closest to Cesare were not spared his vengeance. Francesco Troches, a Spanish confidant in the Borgia's Vatican entourage who was suspected of leaking family plans, fled when he knew Cesare was after him. He was followed, kidnapped, and brought back to Rome, where Cesare had him garrotted and his body thrown into the Tiber. The very same day, a Roman nobleman and papal courtier, Jacopo di Santa Croce, who was believed to have plotted with the Orsini, was executed, and his body dangled from the Sant'Angelo bridge. On Christmas Day Ramiro de Lorqua, Cesare's devoted leader of the Romagna military government was decapitated. His body was left on the ground beside the blood-stained execution block, and his head was lifted up on a lance. Cesare had accused him of corruption, but Ramiro's only crime had been to fall in love with Lucrezia Borgia. Machiavelli suggested that these loyal followers were murdered in such public fashion in order to deter would-be traitors.

13

THE BORGIA HOPES DIE WITH ALEXANDER

Cesare's ruthless genius seemed to have assured his future. After the crushing of the *condotierri* revolt, a string of vital strongholds near Rome were handed over to him by the Orsini family. The aged and blind Cardinal Orsini was arrested and locked up in the Castel Sant'Angelo, where he died some weeks later. Another cardinal, Giovanni Michiel of Venice, died in spring 1503. His estate reverted to the church, which meant Alexander received it. Michiel's servant later claimed that the cardinal had been poisoned by Cesare, on Alexander's orders.

A series of new cardinals were appointed to the Sacred College: all paid handsomely for the privilege, and all were firmly committed to the Borgias. Alexander, at the age of seventy-two, was laying foundations for Cesare's control of the papacy after his death. The pope and his son were both confident – Alexander is recorded as saying: 'What has happened up till now is nothing to that which will soon be seen.' Machiavelli wrote, 'Duke Valentinois exhibits a fortune unheard of, a courage and confidence more than human, believing himself capable of accomplishing whatever he undertakes.'

Cesare had busied himself during the winter when fighting was impossible by recruiting the nucleus of a new army. All the key jobs were assigned to loyal Spaniards, and he ordered that only one *condotierri* lord could field forces at any time. He did not want to risk another rebellious confederation. In July 1503, he announced that he was leaving Rome to join his troops at Perugia, which roused suspicions that he was planning to mount a war of expansion in the Tuscany region.

This would have been suicidal, for King Louis was at that very moment assembling an army of twenty-five thousand men to make another lunge at Naples. However, Cesare was sufficiently aware of the uneasiness surrounding his plans to call in the French ambassador and assure him that he was going to Perugia merely to inspect his army.

The journey was delayed, however, and he was still in the city during the hot Roman August. Fever was rife, and Alexander knew that many earlier popes had died in August. He was in a sombre mood as the twelfth anniversary of his election approached, and when an owl fluttered through a Vatican window to fall dead at his feet, he declared it a bad omen. On August 12, Alexander suddenly fell gravely ill with malaria. Cesare, staying with his father in the holy palace, went down with the same disease, which was spread through the city by a plague of mosquitoes.

For six days, father and son lay ill in adjoining rooms in the Vatican, while doctors tried every possible treatment to cure their fevers. Alexander was bled, and weakened considerably. Cesare was immersed in a giant jar filled with cold water. This treatment nearly proved fatal.

Alexander died on the afternoon of August 18. The news was kept secret while some members of the Borgia family fled Rome and those who remained looted the church treasury. Cesare's follower Miguel di Corella found the cardinal who had the keys to the pope's treasure chest. When the churchman declared himself reluctant to hand over the keys, di Corella threatened to cut the man's throat and toss him out of a window. Di Corella and a bunch of armed cohorts ransacked the papal apartments of all the gold, silver and jewels they could find. They carried off fittings, altar pieces, tabernacles, cups worked in gold and emeralds, a gold statue of a cat with two huge diamonds inset as its eyes, and even the jewel-studded mantle of St Peter. Only when the booty had been carried along the secret tunnel and secreted in the Castel Sant'Angelo were the Vatican doors opened and the pronouncement of death made to the outside world.

Cesare suffered a relapse that same day, and was not

expected to live. But, in the midst of his delirium, he sent orders for his troops to come to Rome, where he would need them during the interregnum. However, French forces commanded by yet another *condotierre*, Francesco Gonzaga, Marchese of Mantua, closed in from their base at Viterbo, forty miles distant. Gonsalvo di Cordova in Naples sent a Spanish force to an encampment within striking distance of Rome.

Johannes Burchard was called to supervise the laying out of the pope's body. Except for a handful of officials and servants, he found the Vatican deserted. The summer heat was decomposing the body rapidly, and Burchard was shocked by its appearance. He later wrote, 'Its face had changed to the colour of mulberry or the blackest cloth, and it was covered in blue-black spots. The nose was swollen, the mouth distended where the tongue was doubled over and the lips seemed to fill everything. The appearance of the face then was more horrifying than anything that had ever been seen or reported before.'

Francesco Gonzaga, who arrived not long after, reported that the body had swollen so much it had lost all human form, and was as broad as it was long: 'The carpenters had made the coffin too narrow and short, so they placed the pope's mitre at his side, rolled up his body in an old carpet, and pummelled and pushed it into the coffin with their fists. No wax tapers or lights were used and no priests or any other persons attended his body.'

The coffin was carried by the traditional band of paupers into St Peter's, where an inexplicable fight broke out amongst palace guards. In the confusion, the pope's body was abandoned. Burchard enlisted the help of some friends to haul the bier to safety behind an iron grill at the back of the altar, where it would be protected from would-be desecrators.

Stories abounded that the evil Alexander had made a pact with the devil to gain the papacy, and that the devil appeared at St Peter's as a black dog to claim the pope's soul. Francesco Gonzaga wrote to his wife, Isabella d'Este, Lucrezia's sister-in-law: 'When he fell sick, he began to talk in such a way that anyone who did not know what was in his mind would have thought that he was wandering, although he was perfectly conscious of what he said. His words were, 'I come, it is right, wait a moment.' Those who know the secret say that in the conclave following the death of Innocent he made a compact with the devil, and purchased the papacy from him at the price of his soul. Among the other provisions of the agreement was one which said that he should be allowed to occupy the Holy See twelve years, and this he did with the addition of four days. There are some who affirm that at the moment he gave up his spirit, seven devils were seen in his chamber.'

The pope's body was in such a bad condition that no-one could be found who was willing to touch even the coffin. So a porter dragged it to the grave with a rope tied round Alexander's feet. His remains were buried in a side chapel of St Peter's, close to the resting places of Pope Calixtus and Alfonso of Bisceglie.

Cesare slowly recovered, but was still too ill to mobilize his forces to meet the adversaries who were threatening to seize his power. Within days of the pope's death, many of the petty tyrants driven out by Cesare were flocking back to regain their feudal lands. Guidobaldo da Montefeltre, Giovanni Sforza, and Pandolfo Malatesta, backed by the Venetians, had walked back into Urbino, Pesaro and Rimini. Gian Paolo Baglioni, who had fortuitously escaped the trap at Senigallia, was reinstated in Perugia. The returning lords of Forlì and Faenza, however, were rebuffed by citizens who preferred the rule of their new master, Cesare.

The Orsini rode into Rome in force to murder Borgia partisans, and to pillage their homes. They wanted Cesare's death, and Giuliano Orsini rode past the heavily guarded palace of San Clemente, into which Cesare had been moved, shouting, 'Let us kill the Jewish dog!'

Some troops loyal to Cesare managed to reach the Castel Sant'Angelo, and two hundred of his knights camped outside the city walls. The Sacred College refused to hold the papal election with Cesare's soldiers at their shoulder, and demanded that he and they withdraw. He eventually agreed to go to the Romagna, provided the cardinals confirmed both his lordship over the captured cities and his position as Captain-General during the interregnum period. This they agreed to, and on September 2 the still weak, emaciated and feverish Cesare was carried out of Rome in a curtained litter. Accompanied by his brother Jofre and mother Vannozza de' Cattanei, he was heading for Nepi to await the results of the election.

From there, he still attempted to influence the voting cardinals, a third of whom were Spaniards and loyal to the Borgia cause. Machiavelli, who had arrived in Rome to observe the election, wrote of Cesare, 'He is more in hopes than ever of doing great things, presupposing that there is a pope according to the wishes of his friends.'

The Borgia arch-enemy, Cardinal Giuliano della Rovere, returned to Rome for the first time since 1497 to make his own bid for the papacy. At the beginning of the conclave he was favourite and he led in the first ballot. However, Cesare swung the crucial Spanish votes behind Cardinal Piccolomini, nephew of Pope Pius II, the family friend who had once shielded Cardinal Rodrigo Borgia.

Piccolomini, who ruled as Pius III, promptly confirmed Cesare Borgia as the church's Captain-General, and ordered the people of the Romagna to remain loyal to their duke. Cesare thus retained his powerful position despite his father's death. However, Pope Pius was aged and frail, too ill even to kneel at his coronation, and it became clear he could not live for very long.

Realizing the need for fast action, Cesare set up a secret deal with King Louis which guaranteed French protection of all his family in exchange for agreed assistance in a forthcoming expedition aimed at throwing the Spaniards out of Naples. Lucrezia also came to her brother's aid when she persuaded Duke Ercole to send one thousand infantrymen, under Spanish commanders, to reinforce the troops Cesare had left under his command, garrisoned at Imola and Cesena.

Cesare, who had returned to Rome to assert his influence on the papal court in person, was waiting for a promised French escort back to the Romagna when Pope Pius became ill. He had recently undergone a leg operation, and was suddenly seized by a fit of vomiting and fever. Soon the whole city knew the old man was dying.

Cesare was in a vulnerable position: the French army was not close enough to help him, the main body of his troops was still in the Romagna, and the pope was on his deathbed and unable to protect him. He decided to march out of Rome with the troops under his direct command. This move was thwarted when two of his Italian infantry companies mutinied, demanding higher pay. His German mercenaries turned on the Italians, and Orsini soldiers rode up to join the confused mêlée. Cesare was still sick and confined to bed, but he heard what was happening. Bellowing 'I would rather die in the saddle than in bed', he rose, mounted his horse, and pitched into the fray. With Jofre at his side, Cesare wielded his sword like a man demented as the battle raged all around St Peter's. Only when he saw that he was hopelessly outnumbered did Cesare order a retreat into the Castel Sant'Angelo. He took with him all the members of his family who were in Rome, including Lucrezia's son Rodrigo, now Duke of Sermoneta, and Alexander's son Giovanni, the 'Infans Romanus', who had been given the Duchy of Spoleto. Also with him went two children, Gerolamo and Camilla, illegitimate children of Cesare's whose mother is unknown.

Pope Pius died on October 17, after a reign of twenty-six days. At the news of his death a mob sacked Cesare's San Clemente palace, and guards were placed on all the gates out of Rome to prevent his escape. Cesare was a prisoner in the city.

Cesare's power in the Romagna had been broken by the returning barons. Only Cesena and Imola and a handful of scattered castles remained loyal. Cesare's last chance was his control of the Spanish cardinals. Giuliano della Rovere, very much the man of the moment, sent an emissary to court Cesare for the votes of the Spaniards. The papacy had been his lifelong ambition and, at sixty, he did not feel he could wait much longer. Della Rovere, a consummate politician, made fulsome promises to Cesare. His lordship over the Romagna states would be acknowledged. He would continue as Captain-General. He could keep all the treasure he had looted from the Vatican. The cardinal had the reputation of being a man of his word, but problems lay ahead for Cesare. On the eve of the conclave, Giuliano confided to an envoy: 'Necessity constrains men to do that which they do not wish, even to place themselves in the hands of others; but once free afterwards, they act in a different manner.'

Della Rovere would probably have won the election nevertheless, but the support of the Spanish cardinals made the result a foregone conclusion, and on November 1, he became Pope Julius II.

At first, it appeared that the new pontiff would stand by his commitments. He wrote to the citizens of Faenza, calling on them to obey Cesare, 'our beloved son, whom we love with a paternal love'. However, the shrewd Machiavelli realized what Pope Julius was doing. He wrote, 'Others, who are no less sagacious, think that, inasmuch as the pontiff had need of the duke in his election, and having made him great promises therefore, he finds it advisable now to feed the duke on hope; and they fear that, if the latter should not decide upon any other course than to remain in Rome, he may be kept there longer than may be agreeable to him; for the pope's innate hatred of him is notorious. And it is not to be supposed that Julius II will so quickly have forgotten the ten years of exile which he had to endure under Pope Alexander VI.'

Cesare was on dangerous ground, and Machiavelli noted, 'The duke lets himself be carried away by that spirited self-confidence of his, and believes that the word of others should be better kept than his own.' The Florentine diplomat considered that Pope Julius 'does not love Valentinois, but nonetheless he strings him along for two reasons: one to keep his word, of which men hold him most observant, and for the obligations he has towards him, being recognizant to him for the good part of the papacy; the other, since it also seems to him, that His Holiness being without forces, the duke is better placed to resist the Venetians.'

In fact, Julius was concerned that the Venetians might seize the power left vacant by Cesare's exit from the Romagna. He considered fulfilling his election promise and sending Cesare to reclaim the cities in the name of the church. But it would have been dangerous to renew Cesare's power, and Julius confided to an envoy: 'We do not wish that he should persuade himself that we will favour him, nor that he shall have even one rampart in the Romagna, and, although we have promised him something, we intend that our promise should extend only to the security of his life and of the money and goods he has stolen.'

Cesare recruited another army, but realized it could not reach the Romagna across country because the route through Umbria was controlled by *condotierri* lords who were now his confirmed enemies. The only other way to the Romagna was by sea to Livorno, then across Tuscany. He requested safe passage through Florentine land from Machiavelli, who saw that Cesare had no prospect of holding the Romagna with the men at his disposal. But Cesare was desperate to regain power – he raged that if he did not get the guarantee of safe conduct, 'he would come to an agreement with the Venetians or with the devil, and he would go to Pisa, and all the money and friends he had left he would employ in doing harm.'

Machiavelli assured Cesare that Florence was considering his request, and urged him to send a negotiator to arrange the details with his ministers. Then he wrote to his governing council: 'I have assured the duke only to give him a bit of hope, that he may not have to delay, and the pope will not therefore have to urge you to give him a safe conduct. Your Lordships, when the duke's man comes, can treat him negligently, and conduct yourselves as you think best.'

Ignoring this reluctance, Cesare sent his cavalry to Ostia, where they sailed for Tuscany. He followed them to the Roman port, where he heard to his anguish that Julius had dismissed him as Captain-General, and the new holder of the post was his old adversary Guidobaldo da Montefeltre, Duke of Urbino.

When news came that the Venetians had, as expected, invaded the Romagna to take Faenza and blockade Imola, the pope saw that he could not hope to hold the region unless he regained possession of the strongholds garrisoned by Borgia troops. So he dispatched an envoy to Ostia, demanding the return of the castles. Cesare refused, and Julius furiously ordered Cesare's arrest. He was brought to Rome in chains and Machiavelli considered that Cesare's refusal meant that he had signed his own death warrant. Rumours quickly spread that Cesare had been killed and thrown into the Tiber. In fact he had been ignominiously locked up in the Borgia apartments from which he and his father had so recently ruled their world. He believed that he was going to die, but seemed unconcerned and passed the days watching his servants gambling, even making jokes about his predicament. One witness said, 'I marvel that a man who is in here can be in such good humour.' When a papal lieutenant asked him the reason for his mood, Cesare replied, 'The more I am in adversity, the more I fortify my spirit.'

Meanwhile, the treasure which Cesare's men had snatched from the Vatican, along with every piece of valuable Borgia property that could be moved, was loaded onto wagons and sent by road to Lucrezia at Ferrara. It never reached her, for it was stolen by war lords on the way.

The two young Borgia dukes who had remained in the Castel Sant'Angelo were smuggled out of Rome by Cardinal Francesco Borgia and taken by a circuitous route to Spain, where they began their education. Vannozza de' Cattanei feared that the pope might be planning to expropriate her home because of her connections with the Borgias, so she donated it to the church of Santa Maria del Popolo, reserving the use of it for herself during her lifetime.

Cesare's imprisonment meant a change of fortune for Dorotea Caracciolo, the Venetian noblewoman he had held prisoner and kept as an unwilling mistress for two years. She was freed from the convent to which Cesare had sent her after Alexander's death, and finally she was happily reunited with her husband.

Cesare had decided that his Romagna fortresses were not much use to him while he was imprisoned, so he tried to buy his freedom by agreeing to hand the castles over to the pope. Envoys were sent from the Vatican to reclaim them, but Cesare's Spanish commanders adamantly refused to relinquish the castles while he was still a prisoner. One of the commanders hung a papal emissary from his castle's ramparts. Cesare was still able to inspire loyalty in his men, despite the fact that he was no longer powerful.

This loyalty produced a violent rage in Julius, who threatened to have Cesare thrown into the Castel Sant'Angelo for the rest of his life. Only the intervention of the cardinals saved him, and the pope incarcerated him in the Hall of the Sibyls instead, the room where Alfonso of Bisceglie had been strangled on Cesare's orders.

When Cesare's garrison commanders threatened to hand their fortresses over to the Venetians, the cardinals advised the pope to let Cesare go free. But then Cesare's immediate hopes were dashed when his advance cavalry was captured in Tuscany by citizens who vividly remembered the looting and pillaging of an earlier Borgia army. He agreed to give Julius written instructions to his commanders, and promised not to enter the Romagna again, and to accept the pope's guarantee of freedom. A galley took Cesare to Ostia, where he was held in the fortress awaiting confirmation that the castles had been handed over. His custodians released him when news of the surrender of the fortresses arrived. Pope Julius sent word that Cesare was not to be freed, but it was too late, and Julius was unable to go back on his word. Cesare quickly fled to Naples, where Gonsalvo di Cordova, now viceroy of an Aragon province, had promised him safe conduct.

Historians have subsequently wondered why Cesare trusted the word of Giuliano della Rovere when he knew how little his own word was worth. After all, the future pope was a longstanding enemy of the Borgias. There are probably two reasons for this: firstly Giuliano had a reputation as an honest man, and Cesare therefore believed his word would bind him. Secondly, Cesare had no choice but to trust him. His own power had been destroyed by the death of Alexander, when he lost the shield of the papacy.

Cesare later told Machiavelli that he had allowed for every possibility except that he himself might be on the point of death when his father died. In *The Prince* Machiavelli holds Cesare up as 'an example to be imitated by all who by fortune and with the arms of others have risen to power', and he was convinced that it was only this totally unforeseen eventuality which prevented the Borgia warrior from extending his rule, possibly throughout Italy. For, if he had been well enough to organize his forces, he might have controlled the papacy while he completed his grand design.

In Naples, Cesare continued to plot how to regain power in the Romagna. He summoned his military captains to his temporary headquarters and spent some of the fortune he had secreted in Genoese and Florentine banks to buy troops, artillery and galleys. This was a breach of the conditions of his welcome, and on May 26, 1504, the eve of his planned departure to begin a new campaign, di Cordova had Cesare arrested and jailed in the Castel Nuovo, a fortress that towered over the city of Naples.

Cesare had become a valuable pawn in international politics. King Ferdinand wanted Pope Julius to grant a dispensation for his daughter, Catherine of Aragon, to marry her dead husband's brother, Henry VIII of England. So the Spanish monarch was happy to sabotage Cesare's planned incursion into the Romagna, but he was not prepared to hand his Borgia hostage over to the pope. He realized it would be useful to keep Cesare for future bargaining.

After the death of Pope Alexander and Cesare's dismissal as Captain-General of the Church, he had outlived his usefulness to the French, who had no further interest in him, and were not prepared to help him. After three months in the Castel Nuovo, Cesare was put aboard a galley bound for

Spain. He disembarked at Villanueva del Grao, the port from which Alonso de Borja, the man who began the Borgia ascent to power, had left Spain sixty-two years before. Under heavy guard, Cesare was imprisoned in the Homage Tower of the fortress of Chinchilla, set amidst the mountains of Valencia. There seemed no possible escape from what was reputed to be the highest tower in the tallest castle in the region. However, Cesare tried to kill the prison governor by throwing him from the parapet, then he tried to get away by shinning down knotted sheets. He fell, fractured his shoulder, and was placed under the strictest surveillance. In mid-summer of 1505, he was transferred to an even more secure prison at the castle of La Mota in central Castile.

Throughout this period, Cesare was still making plans for his future. When Queen Isabella of Aragon died, a civil war between her brother Philip and King Ferdinand seemed likely over the Castilian half of the kingdom. Cesare was earmarked as Philip's chief of staff, but Philip died before the plan could be carried out. Then Cesare planned to make his way to the French court, raise an army, and retake the Romagna.

He managed to escape from La Mota by climbing down a rope provided by a servant whom he had terrified into complicity. A bad fall at the end of his dizzy descent knocked him unconscious, and he had to be held on his horse by his accomplices. By December 1506, Cesare had made his way to Pamplona, capital of Navarre, the tough, independent Basque buffer kingdom set between France and Spain and ruled by his brother-in-law, John d'Albret. It was the first time Cesare had set foot in the city where his appointment as bishop, when he was sixteen years old, had so enraged the population.

He sent jubilant letters to his sister Lucrezia and others, boasting of his escape and his plans for the future, and signing himself 'Cesare Borgia de Francia, Duca di Romagna'. He was scheming to help force the infant Spanish Prince Charles on to the throne of Castile when civil war broke out in Navarre. Taking the field on the side of King

John, with five thousand Basque troops placed under his command, he set up the siege of the frontier hill town of Viana, where a rebel lord, Luis de Beaumonte, defiantly flew the flag of King Ferdinand. On March 11, 1507, he was lured alone into an ambush, hauled from his horse, and hacked to death. His naked and bloody body, covered with twenty-five wounds, was testimony to the fierce resistance he had made.

King John had Cesare's body buried in the simple parish church of Santa Maria in Viana. The inscription on his tomb attested to the effect which the thirty-one-year-old warrior had had on his world: 'Here, in a scant piece of earth, lies he whom all the world feared.' A French soldier who had served with him added his own assessment: 'Of his virtues I shall say no more, for they have been talked about enough, but I must say he was a good comrade and a brave man.'

14

LUCREZIA AND THE LEGACY OF THE BORGIAS

Lucrezia had been devastated by the news of her father's death – she draped her rooms in black and felt that she, too, was dying. Her position became vulnerable when King Louis of France suggested that, as a family link with the Borgias was no longer of any value, Alfonso d'Este should divorce his wife. Louis wrote to Duke Ercole, 'I know that you were never satisfied with this marriage; this Madonna Lucrezia is not Don Alfonso's real wife.'

Alfonso d'Este had never been in love with Lucrezia, and was more interested in artillery – he often went on trips to inspect new cannons, and used these journeys to cover up the fact that he was seeing one of his mistresses. His indifference made Lucrezia cling to Adriana del Mila and the ladies-in-waiting who had joined her from Rome, and she sacked most of her Ferrarese staff. The duke then pared her household allowance, so she was obliged to pawn some of her jewels to keep up appearances. Lucrezia did, however, become friendly with a Sienese girl called Niccola, who was in love with Lucrezia's brother-in-law, Ferrante.

During her first pregnancy, Lucrezia had been weakened by a persistent fever, and she gave birth to a stillborn baby. The doctors had been so worried by the frailty of Lucrezia's condition that they told her at first that the child was alive. Lucrezia's pulse was so weak at one time that she cried, 'Oh, God, I'm dead', and made out a will. However, she recovered eventually. During her illness, Alfonso sat reluctantly at her bedside, but when Lucrezia was well enough, he excused himself to visit a distant shrine and give thanks for her renewed health. Lucrezia's second pregnancy ended in a miscarriage after a particularly hectic night of dancing.

A woman of artistic refinement, a lover of music and poetry, Lucrezia did not love her husband. She had an affair with a Venetian poet, Pietro Bembo, who was living in Ferrara. Lucrezia was twenty-three when they met, and he dedicated poems and songs to her beauty and elegance. Love letters, unsigned and in code, flowed between them, and Lucrezia sent Pietro a lock of her hair. Even though Alfonso's interest in Lucrezia was limited, he did not like the idea of being cuckolded. So he built a secret passage between his apartment and Lucrezia's so he could watch her. However this did not prevent Pietro rushing to Lucrezia's side when news came of her father's death.

At the beginning of 1505, Duke Ercole died. Alfonso acceded to the title and Lucrezia became duchess. Meanwhile she desperately wanted another child: she missed her absent son Rodrigo and wanted a male heir to Alfonso who would sit on the throne and secure the dynasty. That year she gave birth to a boy, Alessandro, only weeks after being stunned by her father's death. The child was so weak that he survived only a few days.

A friar informed Lucrezia of Cesare's subsequent death in Navarre, but Lucrezia took the news calmly, perhaps remembering that Cesare had ordered the garrotting of her second husband. 'The more I try to follow God's will, the more he visits me with sorrow', she said, and retired to a convent for two days to mourn her brother's death in private.

Just over a year later, Lucrezia gave birth to a healthy son, Ercole, the future Duke of Ferrara, and the event was celebrated in a carnival atmosphere. Her father-in-law was ecstatic, and Lucrezia's position was secured. At the same time, she had taken a new lover – Francesco Gonzaga, the Marchese of Mantua, husband of her hated sister-in-law Isabella. She took particular delight in the liaison, which continued for some years, because she saw it as revenge on Isabella. Gonzaga was a famed soldier and a renowned womanizer who swept Lucrezia off her feet.

Francesco Gonzaga was appointed to Cesare's old position as Captain-General of the Church by Pope Julius, who threw him into battle against his brother-in-law Duke Alfonso d'Este. The duke had sided with France against the papacy, and Gonzaga's papal army was sent to besiege Ferrara. The Marchese dreamed of hounding Alfonso out of the city, snatching Lucrezia, and carrying her off to Mantua as his mistress. So confident of success was he that he even had rooms prepared for her. However, the French arrived in force and drove off the invading army.

Lucrezia began to devote herself to the governance of Ferrara, which she undertook as regent during Duke Alfonso's frequent journeys for war or state affairs. She heard the complaints and received the petitions of the ordinary people, and became very popular as a result. She also brought to the royal court of Ferrara a charm, gaiety and sophistication which had previously been lacking. She also founded convents and hospitals, and joined the Third Order of Saint Francis, which allowed lay members to live in the outside world while also belonging to a convent.

She had four more healthy children, three sons, Ippolito, Alessandro and Francesco, and a daughter Eleanora. Lucrezia's half-brother Giovanni, the 'Infans Romanus', joined her household for a short while before moving on to the French court. Indolent and capricious, and heir to estates in Valencia though he had lost his title as Duke of Nepi, Giovanni died in France while still a young man. Cesare's two mysterious illegitimate children, Camilla and Gerolamo, were also sent to Ferrara to be brought up under Lucrezia's protection. In contrast to her father Camilla became a nun with a great reputation for saintliness. She eventually became abbess of the Ferrarese convent of Corpo di Christo, and died there in 1573. Gerolamo lived in the ducal household at Ferrara and later married a daughter of the lord of Capri. His temperament seems to have been more like his father's, for he is reputed to have stabbed to death one of Cesare's old enemies.

Lucrezia never again saw Rodrigo, her own son by Alfonso

of Bisceglie, and he died in 1512. News of the death of her mother, Vannozza de' Cattanei, reached Lucrezia in November 1518. The seventy-six-year-old woman was buried close to her second son Juan, the Duke of Gandia, in the church of Santa Maria del Popolo. Her funeral was attended by every member of the Sacred College on the express order of Julius's successor, Pope Leo X, who as Giovanni de' Medici had been made a cardinal when a boy by Alexander. Vannozza donated all her jewels to the church. She had survived each of her husbands and all of her children except for Lucrezia. Some months later, Lucrezia heard that Francesco Gonzaga had also died.

At the age of thirty-eight, Lucrezia became pregnant for the eleventh time. She gave birth to a daughter who was so frail that she was immediately baptized, as Isabella Maria. It was a difficult birth, and Lucrezia became feverish soon afterwards. Doctors cut off all her hair in a macabre attempt to save her life. Alfonso ordered prayers and a religious procession as he watched at his wife's bedside.

Lucrezia died on June 23, 1519. She was buried in a simple tomb at Ferrara, and Alfonso fainted at her funeral. His belated feelings for Lucrezia were expressed in a letter announcing her death which he wrote to a relative: 'It has just pleased Our Lord to summon unto himself the soul of the illustrious lady the Duchess, my dear wife. I cannot write this without tears, knowing myself to be deprived of such a dear and sweet companion. For such her exemplary conduct and the tender love which existed between us made her to me.'

Some of Lucrezia's children married into Italian and French noble families, but the Ferrarese ducal line was ended when the state was claimed by the church. Her son Ippolito d'Este followed the Borgia family tradition and entered the church; he became a cardinal. Her only surviving brother, Jofre, who had been widowed by the death of Princess Sancia in 1506, signed up as a soldier under Gonsalvo di Cordova in Naples. He died in obscurity in 1516, aged thirty-five, but his children married into the Neapolitan and Aragon royal houses, and a grandson was responsible for founding the village of Borgia in 1547.

Maria Enriquez, widow of the dissolute Juan Borgia, Duke of Gandia, became a nun. The couple's descendants carried the Borgia name through Spanish history as soldiers, ambassadors and cardinals. Francis Borgia, a grandson of Juan Borgia, accompanied Charles V of Aragon on military campaigns. Appalled at the barbarity of army life he became a priest, then a Jesuit, and finally the third general of the Jesuit order. He was canonized in 1671 as St Francis. His eldest son governed Spain's colony of New Granada in South America for two decades, and the dukes of Gandia survived into the 19th century.

The great-great-grandson of Alexander's daughter Isabella Matuzzi became Pope Innocent X, and other Borgias figured in the Sacred College and the Italian nobility for centuries. Cardinal Stefano Borgia, for example, was a leading but unsuccessful papal candidate in the conclave of 1799.

When Cesare's wife, Charlotte d'Albret, heard of his death she plunged herself into an obsessional mourning for the rest of her life, in memory of a man she had known for only a few short months. Her chateau home was draped in black crepe, she ate off black plates, slept between black sheets, and even her daughter Luisa's pony was clad in black. Luisa, who had never met her father, married a French nobleman. He was killed in battle, but with her second husband she had a family. Today's counts of Busset and Chalus are thus the direct heirs, through Luisa, of Cesare Borgia.

Julius II, the Borgia's antagonist, became a great Renaissance pope, leaving his mark on Rome and the church with Michelangelo's Sistine Chapel and Raphael's masterpiece, the Stanze della Segnatura, in the Vatican. He also commissioned Michelangelo and Bramante to start work on the new basilica of St Peter's. A statue of Moses by Michelangelo guards Julius's tomb in his cardinalate parish church of San Pietro in Vincoli.

Pope Julius villified the name of the family who had dominated so much of his life. Cardinal Francesco Borgia, who continued the family feud by attempting to have Julius deposed, was himself stripped of his cardinalate, and died of apoplexy. However, Alexander's daughter by Giulia Farnese, Laura, later married into the della Rovere family.

It was Julius who ordered that the Borgia apartments in the Vatican should be sealed. The fearsome legend of the evil family, fuelled to a great extent by Julius, meant that the rooms were to remain closed for over three hundred years. Now they have become a great tourist attraction.

The remains of Alexander and Calixtus, the Borgia popes, were removed from St Peter's and taken to the Spanish church of Santa Maria de Monserrato, where they were placed in a box bearing the simple epitaph, 'The bones of two popes lie in this chest, and they are Calixtus III and Alexander VI, and they were Spaniards.'

The insidious attacks on the Borgia name had begun during Alexander's papacy: the family was hated for its success, as well as for its methods. The Italians feared the Borgias as a Spanish Mafia in their midst, and this they truly were.

They were ambitious, fearless and unscrupulous, but they were not the evil brood of monstrous, murdering adventurers, poisoning their way to power, as history has indicted them. Murder was common among the ruling families of Italy – in one internecine massacre, half the Baglioni family of Perugia were murdered in their beds. Rome was a city full of brutal and unsolved murders, and it was easy for the scandal-mongers to lay the blame at the Borgia door. Murders *were* committed on Borgia orders, particularly on behalf of Cesare, who operated like a gangster. However, their motive was always political. But the Borgias were not responsible for most of the crimes attributed to them. Corruption in the church was endemic long before the ascendancy of the Borgia popes.

The most scandalous claim made against the Borgias and passed down through history is that Lucrezia slept with her father and brothers, and that she poisoned her three husbands. In fact, Lucrezia was a pawn in the family dynastic schemes. Victor Hugo's play *Lucrezia Borgia* features these allegations as does Donizetti's opera of the same name, which also shows Lucrezia continuing her debauchery in Ferrara and poisoning more hapless victims.

Pope Alexander VI dominated his world with his personality and was one of the most able diplomats to occupy the papal throne. He was also the most outrageous of popes, his debauchery bringing unprecedented scandal to the church. The evils associated with his reign weakened the church's moral authority and this contributed to its problems in the Protestant Reformation.

As for Alexander's dream of a united Italy, with his son as king: Machiavelli believed that the partnership of Alexander and Cesare could have achieved this, given time. Alexander's attempts to aggrandize his family tamed the Romagna barons, but the Borgia use of foreign power in Italy saw the division of the state of Naples between France and Spain. The squabble over the spoils ended in a truce, with Naples left in Spanish hands as a colony. The open door to Italy remained, and this led eventually to the sacking of Rome by French troops in 1527. The dream of Italian unification was shelved, this time for over three hundred years.

Evidence of Cesare's brief, frenetic years of power can be seen at Forli, his last stronghold. There Cesare's coat-of-arms, with the Borgia bull alongside the lilies of France and the batons of the Captain-General of the Church, is barely visible on the walls, almost effaced by time. At Senigallia, where he trapped the *condotierri* rebels, a square has been named 'Piazza del Duca'.

His only notable memorial is a bronze bust erected in 1965 in a quiet square in Viana, Navarre, now part of Spain. His bones were reburied in a place of honour near the front of the church of Santa Maria, and a marble tablet over them bears this inscription: 'Cesare Borgia, Generalissimo of the Navarrese and pontifical armies, died in the fields of Viana, March 11, 1507.' Ironically enough, Cesare is regarded in Navarre as a selfless hero of the fight for Basque independence. What would that ruthless, cunning soldier-of-fortune, the illegitimate son of a pope, have thought of such an epitaph?

Also in Hamlyn Paperbacks

Harry Edgington

PRINCE REGENT

In his youth he was the playboy prince, the darling of society, but behind a façade of elegance and taste, George IV turned his life into an orgy lasting half a century. Bloated with drink, he lurched from bed to bed, casting off his mistresses with spoilt abandon.

With a mass of detailed research, Harry Edgington reveals the truth about a King who finally dared not show his face for fear of public insult. For Prinny's debauched affairs shocked society, even in those permissive days. His official marriage to Caroline of Brunswick was a disaster — he even tried to have her imprisoned. But one woman did succeed in capturing his heart and hand — the Catholic widow, Mrs Fitzherbert. They married secretly and she remained the mysterious love of his life.

This is the scandalous story of a royal rake – the private life of George IV.

Also in Hamlyn Paperbacks

Harry Edgington

NELSON

The diminutive figure of Vice-Admiral Horatio Nelson towered over the world. He was a fearless warrior, whose victories at the Nile, Copenhagen and Trafalgar doomed Napoleon's empire and assured his own immortality.

But Nelson's life was equally dominated by his weakness for women. He was as bold in love as he was in battle – a series of all-consuming romances ended only briefly when he married. Then fate engineered a meeting with Emma, Lady Hamilton, the most notorious woman of her day, an adventuress who was to dominate his existence. The scandal of his brazen *ménage à trois* with Emma and her husband, Sir William Hamilton, haunted his last years.

Nelson died as victory at Trafalgar was announced and England was stunned with grief. His rejected wife, and her arch rival, Lady Hamilton, led the country in mourning one of her greatest sons.

NON-FICTION

GENERAL

☐ Guide to the Channel Islands	J. Anderson & E. Swinglehurst	90p
☐ The Complete Traveller	Joan Bakewell	£1.95
☐ Time Out London Shopping Guide	Lindsey Bareham	£1.50
☐ The Black Angels	Rupert Butler	£1.35
☐ Hand of Steel	Rupert Butler	£1.35
☐ A Walk Around the Lakes	Hunter Davies	£1.50
☐ Truly Murderous	John Dunning	95p
☐ Shocktrauma	J. Franklin & A. Doelp	£1.25
☐ Hitler's Secret Life	Glenn B. Infield	£1.25
☐ Wing Leader	Johnnie Johnson	£1.50
☐ Me, to Name but a Few	Spike Mullins	£1.25
☐ The Complete Book of Cleaning	Barty Phillips	£1.00
☐ The Devil's Bedside Book	Leonard Rossiter	£1.50
☐ The Fugu Plan	M. Tokayer & M. Swartz	85p
☐ Mike Yarwood's Family Joke Book	Mike Yarwood	£1.75
		85p

BIOGRAPHY/AUTOBIOGRAPHY

☐ Go-Boy	Roger Caron	£1.25
☐ The Queen Mother Herself	Helen Cathcart	£1.25
☐ George Stephenson	Hunter Davies	£1.50
☐ The Queen's Children	Donald Edgar	£1.25
☐ The Admiral's Daughter	Victoria Fyodorova	£1.50
☐ All of Me	Rose Neighbour	£1.00
☐ Biggles: The Authorized Biography	John Pearson	£1.50
☐ Tell Me Who I am Before I Die	C. Peters with T. Schwarz	£1.00
☐ Kiss	John Swenson	95p

HEALTH/SELF-HELP/POCKET HEALTH GUIDES

☐ The Hamlyn Family First Aid Book	Dr. Robert Andrew	£1.50
☐ The Babysitter Book	J. Curry & J. Cunningham	£1.25
☐ The Pick of Woman's Own Diets	Jo Foley	95p
☐ Woman X Two	Mary Kenny	£1.10
☐ Cystitis: A Complete Self-help Guide	Angela Kilmartin	£1.00
☐ Fat is a Feminist Issue	Susie Orbach	95p
☐ Related to Sex	Claire Rayner	£1.25
☐ The Working Woman's Body Book	L. Rowen with B. Winkler	95p
☐ Natural Sex	Mary Shivanandan	£1.25
☐ Woman's Own Birth Control	Dr. Michael Smith	£1.25
☐ Allergies	Robert Eagle	65p
☐ Arthritis and Rheumatism	Dr. Luke Fernandes	65p
☐ Back Pain	Dr. Paul Dudley	65p
☐ Migraine	Dr. Finlay Campbell	65p
☐ Pre-Menstrual Tension	June Clark	65p
☐ Skin Troubles	Deanna Wilson	65p

REFERENCE

☐ The Sunday Times Guide to Movies on Television	A. & E. Allan	£1.50
☐ The Cheiro Book of Fate and Fortune	Cheiro	£1.50
☐ Hunter Davies's Book of British Lists	Hunter Davies	£1.25
☐ What's Wrong with your Pet?	Hugo Kerr	95p
☐ Caring for Cats and Kittens	John Montgomery	95p
☐ Collecting for Profit	Sam Richards	£1.25
☐ Questions of Law	Bill Thomas	95p

GAMES & PASTIMES

☐ The Hamlyn Book of Brainteasers and Mindbenders	Ben Hamilton	85p
☐ The Celebrity Quiz Book	Bob Monkhouse	95p
☐ The Hamlyn Book of Crosswords 5		70p
☐ The Hamlyn Book of Wordways 1		75p
☐ The Hamlyn Family Quiz Book		85p

FICTION

GENERAL

☐ Chains	Justin Adams	£1.25
☐ Secrets	F. Lee Bailey	£1.25
☐ The Last Liberator	John Clive	£1.25
☐ Wyndward Passion	Norman Daniels	£1.35
☐ Rich Little Poor Girl	Terence Feely	£1.50
☐ Abingdon's	Michael French	£1.25
☐ The Moviola Man	Bill and Colleen Mahan	£1.25
☐ Running Scared	Gregory Mcdonald	85p
☐ Gossip	Marc Olden	£1.25
☐ The Red Raven	Lilli Palmer	£1.25
☐ The Sounds of Silence	Judith Richards	£1.00
☐ Summer Lightning	Judith Richards	£1.25
☐ The Hamptons	Charles Rigdon	£1.35
☐ The Affair of Nina B.	Simmel	95p
☐ The Berlin Connection	Simmel	£1.50
☐ The Cain Conspiracy	Simmel	£1.20
☐ Double Agent—Triple Cross	Simmel	£1.35
☐ Celestial Navigation	Anne Tyler	£1.00
☐ Searching for Caleb	Anne Tyler	£1.00

WESTERN BLADE SERIES

☐ No. 1 The Indian Incident	Matt Chisholm	75p
☐ No. 2 The Tucson Conspiracy	Matt Chisholm	75p
☐ No. 3 The Laredo Assignment	Matt Chisholm	75p
☐ No. 4 The Pecos Manhunt	Matt Chisholm	75p
☐ No. 5 The Colorado Virgins	Matt Chisholm	85p
☐ No. 6 The Mexican Proposition	Matt Chisholm	85p
☐ No. 7 The Arizona Climax	Matt Chisholm	85p
☐ No. 8 The Nevada Mustang	Matt Chisholm	85p
☐ No. 9 The Montana Deadlock	Matt Chisholm	85p
☐ No. 10 The Cheyenne Trap	Matt Chisholm	95p
☐ No. 11 The Navaho Trail	Matt Chisholm	95p

WAR

☐ The Andersen Assault	Peter Leslie	£1.25
☐ Killers Under a Cruel Sky	Peter Leslie	£1.25
☐ Jenny's War	Jack Stoneley	£1.25

NAVAL HISTORICAL

☐ HMS Bounty	John Maxwell	£1.00
☐ The Mary Celeste	John Maxwell	£1.00
☐ The Baltic Convoy	Showell Styles	95p

SCIENCE FICTION

☐ Clash by Night	Henry Kuttner	95p
☐ Drinking Sapphire Wine	Tanith Lee	£1.25
☐ Journey	Marta Randall	£1.00

NON-FICTION

GENERAL COOKERY

- [ ] **Hints for Modern Cooks** — Audrey Ellis — £1.00
- [ ] **Comprehensive Guide to Deep Freezing** — 65p
- [ ] **Home Made Country Wines** — 50p
- [ ] **Indian Cooking** — A. Hosain & S. Pasricha — £1.50
- [ ] **Salads the Year Round** — Joy Larkcom — £1.25

KITCHEN LIBRARY SERIES

- [ ] **Know Your Onions** — Kate Hastrop — 95p
- [ ] **Home Preserving and Bottling** — Gladys Mann — 80p
- [ ] **Home Baked Breads and Cakes** — Mary Norwak — 75p
- [ ] **Easy Icing** — Marguerite Patten — 85p
- [ ] **Wine Making at Home** — Francis Pinnegar — 80p
- [ ] **Mixer and Blender Cookbook** — Myra Street — 80p
- [ ] **Pasta Cookbook** — Myra Street — 75p
- [ ] **The Hamlyn Pressure Cookbook** — Jane Todd — 85p

GARDENING/HOBBIES

- [ ] **Restoring Old Junk** — Michèle Brown — 75p
- [ ] **A Vegetable Plot for Two or More** — D. B. Clay Jones — £1.00
- [ ] **Greenhouse Gardening** — Sue Phillips — £1.25
- [ ] **'Jock' Davidson's House Plant Book** — £1.25

GENERAL

- [ ] **Guide to the Channel Islands** — J. Anderson & E. Swinglehurst — 90p
- [ ] **The Complete Traveller** — Joan Bakewell — £1.95
- [ ] **Time Out London Shopping Guide** — Lindsey Bareham — £1.50
- [ ] **The Black Angels** — Rupert Butler — £1.35
- [ ] **Hand of Steel** — Rupert Butler — £1.35
- [ ] **A Walk Around the Lakes** — Hunter Davies — £1.50
- [ ] **Truly Murderous** — John Dunning — 95p
- [ ] **Shocktrauma** — J. Franklin & A. Doelp — £1.25
- [ ] **Hitler's Secret Life** — Glenn B. Infield — £1.50
- [ ] **Wing Leader** — Johnnie Johnson — £1.25
- [ ] **Me, to Name but a Few** — Spike Mullins — £1.00
- [ ] **The Complete Book of Cleaning** — Barty Phillips — £1.50
- [ ] **The Devil's Bedside Book** — Leonard Rossiter — 85p
- [ ] **The Fugu Plan** — M. Tokayer & M. Swartz — £1.75
- [ ] **Mike Yarwood's Family Joke Book** — Mike Yarwood — 85p

HEALTH/SELF-HELP/POCKET HEALTH GUIDES

- [ ] **The Babysitter Book** — J. Curry & J. Cunningham — £1.25
- [ ] **The Pick of Woman's Own Diets** — Jo Foley — 95p
- [ ] **Woman X Two** — Mary Kenny — £1.10
- [ ] **Cystitis: A Complete Self-help Guide** — Angela Kilmartin — £1.00
- [ ] **Fat is a Feminist Issue** — Susie Orbach — 95p
- [ ] **Related to Sex** — Claire Rayner — £1.25
- [ ] **The Working Woman's Body Book** — L. Rowen with B. Winkler — 95p

NAME ....

ADDRESS..

....

Write to Hamlyn Paperbacks Cash Sales, PO Box 11, Falmouth, Cornwall TR10 9EN.

Please indicate order and enclose remittance to the value of the cover price plus:

U.K.: Please allow 40p for the first book, 18p for the second book and 13p for each additional book ordered, to a maximum charge of £1.49.

B.F.P.O. & EIRE: Please allow 40p for the first book, 18p for the second book plus 13p per copy for the next 7 books, thereafter 7p per book.

OVERSEAS: Please allow 60p for the first book plus 18p per copy for each additional book.

Whilst every effort is made to keep prices low it is sometimes necessary to increase cover prices and also postage and packing rates at short notice. Hamlyn Paperbacks reserve the right to show new retail prices on covers which may differ from those previously advertised in the text or elsewhere.